You can build great online stores with Magento.

We've met lots of different types of Magento learners:

- Magento learners come from many different backgrounds. They are accountants, florists, photographers, secretaries, factory workers, stay-at-home parents, and people from all walks of life.

- Magento learners don't need to know anything about websites. Some Magento learners are professional web designers, but many others have never built a site before and don't know any website code or jargon.

- Magento learners don't need any experience. We've trained people who went to work the previous week and found their boss saying, "Surprise! You're running our Magento site!" They often still wore their look of surprise.

- Magento learners are of all ages. We've taught 15-year old students skipping class all the way up to retirees in their '80s.

If any of those descriptions sound like you, you've picked up the right book.

Using plain English and straightforward instructions, this book will help teach you how to build great websites using Magento.

## THIS BOOK IS ACTIVE

You don't learn to ride a bicycle by reading a book: You learn by actually riding.

You don't learn to drive a car by reading a book: You learn by actually driving.

A book can help and give some advice, but without actually riding a bike or driving a car, you'll never really learn. The same is true with Magento.

So, throughout every chapter of this book, you're going to be asked to work with Magento.

## THIS BOOK USES SPECIFIC EXAMPLES

After you master the techniques in this book, you can build your own websites for companies, charities, schools, sports, or whatever else you need.

However, this book uses a specific example site. Asking all the readers of this book to build the same site makes it easy for us to give you specific instructions, explanations, and screenshots.

It's not essential that you follow every task provided, but by following the flow of each chapter, you can get a good understanding of all the key Magento concepts.

The example we're going to use is an online store called "Orangeville". You're going to create a store full of orange-colored products. That's going to be the project you use to see how to build and run a Magento site.

## THIS BOOK WILL LEAVE SOME THINGS OUT

Big books are no fun. They're expensive to buy, heavy to carry, and often written in long, complicated sentences, paragraphs, and chapters that go on and on while the text grows and the words grow longer and more obscure as the author tries to show their verbosity and vocabulary, examining the thesaurus for words that describe, narrate, impress, and fill up space but never quite get to the point so that you end up going back to the beginning of the long confusing text and try to reread, but then you start wondering what's for dinner or what's on TV instead.

Yes, this book will also include some bad jokes.

This book is as small as possible because it leaves things out.

You're going to read that time and time again, but it's worth repeating: This book will leave things out.

You will focus on only the most important parts of Magento so that you can understand them as easily as possible.

This book is not comprehensive. It does not contain everything you could know about Magento. It contains only what a Magento beginner needs to know.

## THIS BOOK USES ALMOST NO CODE

You do not need to know any HTML and CSS to use this book. That is a deliberate decision because we want to make this book accessible to ordinary people. We believe you don't have to be a developer to use Magento.

However, that will disappoint some of you because this book does not discuss designing themes or building modules. If you do know CSS and PHP and want to dive into more advanced topics, there's a lot of advanced training at https://ostraining.com/classes/magento.

## THINGS IN THIS BOOK WILL CHANGE

Magento changes regularly, and so do the extra features and designs that you add on to it.

Everything in this book is correct at the time of writing. However, it's possible that some of the instructions and screen shots may become out-of-date.

Be patient with any changes you find. If you find any changes, email us at books@ostraining.com.

## WHAT DO YOU NEED FOR THIS BOOK?

Now that you know a little bit about this book, let's make sure you're ready to follow along.

You need only two things to follow along with the exercises in this book:

- A computer with an Internet connection
- A hosting account or computer where you can install Magento

However, before you start, you probably need to know something about Magento. Turn to Chapter 1 and let's get started!

## ABOUT OSTRAINING

Magento 2 Explained is one of a series of books from OSTraining.

As readers and writers, we wanted a new way to publish books.

Old-fashioned paperback books are often out-of-date and expensive.

Books from OSTraining are constantly updated, and affordable. If you join the OSTraining Book Club, you can get access to many books for the price of one.

Find out more: https://ostraining.com/books.

Use the coupon "**magento2explained**" to save 35% on your membership.

## ABOUT NEXCESS

Magento 2 Explained was made possible by the support of Nexcess.net. Their Magento hosting is at https://www.nexcess.net/magento/hosting.

### EXPERIENCE BEYOND.

New technology comes with a promise. Almost 20 years ago, from a small garage in Michigan, we set out to fulfill that promise: to become a hosting provider that empowers clients to create and grow the businesses they want.

Now, from our Michigan headquarters, we hold data centers around the world that offer the best in terms of performance, reliability, and control.

By embracing complexity, providing stability, and working with our clients, partners, and team members, we've managed to create innovations that have changed the face of web hosting support and management forever.

Experience the promise of technology with Nexcess.

TOGETHER WE CAN DO IT BETTER.

We've had over 17 years to polish our team and technology. We promise performance and support beyond what you've come to expect from the industry. We deliver on that promise by fine-tuning our performance-optimized infrastructure to your needs. Whether you're a Magento merchant, a growing enterprise, or a blogging fanatic, Nexcess Cloud solutions are built to help you outperform the competition. Your success is our success, let's grow and succeed together.

## UNRIVALED SUPPORT

We're proud of what we do and love providing unmatched support 24 hours a day, 365 days a year. Our dedicated Support Team and Enterprise Support Group (ESG) work together to not only fix problems but to prevent them before they arise.

## VETERANS IN ECOMMERCE

We currently manage and support more than 40,000 merchants around the globe. All benefit from an eCommerce-optimized infrastructure, designed to deliver unparalleled security, scalability, and performance.

## SECURE AND RELIABLE PERFORMANCE

The Nexcess Cloud runs on a combination of optimized software and top-of-the-line hardware, all managed within our secure state-of-the-art data centers. Merchants expect and deserve reliable and rapid performance from their stores. Give your customers a seamless experience with eCommerce-optimized cloud hosting, and convert a great first impression into repeat business.

## BEYOND SIMPLE MIGRATION

If you're considering changing hosts but are overwhelmed by the logistics of moving your site, leave it to us. Our dedicated migrations team will manage all the details of the move for you, with little to no downtime. If we require your input, we'll guide you every step of the way. No frustration, just seamless migration. We will:

• Transfer all site data.
• Synchronize database content.
• Assist with email issues or misdelivery.
• Arrange a time to change DNS information.

## ABOUT THE OSTRAINING TEAM

I have split my career between teaching and web development. In 2007, I combined the two by starting to teach web development and established OSTraining. Through our books and videos, OSTraining has taught 100,000's of people to build websites with open source software. I am originally from England, and now live in Florida.

Magento 2 Explained would not be possible without the help of the OSTraining team, especially Valentín García who designed the cover and several of the illustrations used in this book.

Thanks also to my wife, Stacey. She has saved me from many mistakes over the years, and many terrible typos in this book.

# WE OFTEN UPDATE THIS BOOK

## THIS BOOK WILL CHANGE

We aim to keep this book up-to-date, and so regularly release new versions to keep up with changes in Magento. This is version 2.1 of Magento 2 Explained and was published on August 1, 2018.

If you find anything that is out-of-date, please email us at books@ostraining.com. We'll update the book, and to say thank you, we'll provide you with a new copy.

We often release updates for this book. Most of the time, frequent updates are wonderful. If Magento makes a change in the morning, we can have a new version of this book available in the afternoon. Most traditional publishers wait years and years before updating their books.

There are two disadvantages to be aware of:

- Page numbers do change. We often add and remove material from the book to reflect changes in Magento.
- There's no index at the back of this book. This is because page numbers do change, and also because our self-publishing platform doesn't have a way to create indexes yet. We hope to find a solution for that soon.

Hopefully, you think that the advantages outweigh the disadvantages. If you have any questions, we're always happy to chat: books@ostraining.com.

## ARE YOU AN AUTHOR?

---

If you enjoy writing about the web, we'd love to talk with you.

Most publishing companies are slow, boring, inflexible and don't pay very well.

Here at OSTraining, we try to be different:

- **Fun**: We use modern publishing tools that make writing books as easy as blogging.
- **Fast**: We move quickly. Some books get written and published in less than a month.
- **Flexible**: It's easy to update your books. If technology changes in the morning, you can update your book by the afternoon.
- **Fair**: Profits from the books are shared 50/50 with the author.

Do you have a topic you'd love to write about? We publish books on almost all web-related topics.

Whether you want to write a short 100-page overview, or a comprehensive 500-page guide, we'd love to hear from you.

Contact us via email: books@ostraining.com.

## ARE YOU A TEACHER?

---

Many schools, colleges and organizations have adopted OSTraining books as a teaching guide.

This book is designed to be a step-by-step guide that students can follow at different speeds. The book can be used for a one-day class, or a longer class over multiple weeks.

If you are interested in using Magento 2 Explained in your class, we'd be delighted to help you with review copies, and all the advice you need.

Please email books@ostraining.com to talk with us.

## SPONSOR AN OSTRAINING BOOK

Is your company interested in sponsoring an OSTraining book?

Our books are some of the world's best-selling guides to the software they cover.

People love to read our books and learn about new web design topics.

Why not reach those people? Partner with us to showcase your company to thousands of web developers.

We have partnered with Acquia, Pantheon, Nexcess, GoDaddy, InMotion, GlowHost and Ecwid to provide sponsored training to millions of people.

If you want to learn more, visit https://ostraining.com/ sponsor or email us at books@ostraining.com.

## WE WANT TO HEAR FROM YOU

Are you satisfied with your purchase of Magento 2 Explained? Let us know and help us reach others who would benefit from this book.

We encourage you to share your experience. Here are two ways you can help:

- Leave your review on Amazon's product page of Magento 2 Explained.

- Email your review to books@ostraining.com.

Thanks for reading Magento 2 Explained. We wish you the best in your future endeavors with Magento.

## THE LEGAL DETAILS

# MAGENTO 2 EXPLAINED

STEPHEN BURGE

*OSTraining*

# CONTENTS

# MAGENTO EXPLAINED

Before you start using Magento, let's give you some background on Magento itself.

In this chapter, we'll explain what Magento is and where it came from. We'll also tell you who owns Magento and who uses it. Finally, we'll explain why you should use Magento and which version of the software you should choose.

## WHAT IS MAGENTO?

Magento is ecommerce software.

It's designed for people to create powerful online stores.

Magento is normally used by medium-to-large stores. Most Magento stores have revenue of over $100,000 per year. If you are looking for ecommerce software that's quick and easy to use, there are better alternatives, including Shopify and Ecwid. Magento's target audience is larger companies with more complex requirements.

## A BRIEF HISTORY OF MAGENTO

Magento was created by a company called Varien from Los Angeles, led by Roy Rubin and Yoav Kutner.

In the mid-2000's, they had been working with an ecommerce platform called osCommerce. After becoming frustrated with the limitation of osCommerce, Roy and Yoav decided to create their own version of the software. However, after several months of work, they decided to leave osCommerce behind entirely and write a new system.

The first public beta of their new software arrived August 2007.

Version 1.0 was released in March 2008 and was immediately popular. Not only was Magento completely free to use, but it also used the latest technology at a time when some rivals were stuck with older code. Within a year, Magento was more popular than osCommerce.

Varien was a company and so needed to make money from their invention. In 2009, they launched "Magento Enterprise Edition", which cost $10,000. The Enterprise version had additional features for high-end users and came with support directly from Varien.

In 2010, eBay purchased 49% of Varien, and then took over the company entirely in 2013. It's fair to say that Magento stagnated inside the much larger company, and it was sold to a private equity firm in 2015.

The new owners of Magento breathed new life into the project, with a wide range of new investments and initiatives. A successful new version of Magento was released, which they called Magento 2.

In May 2018, Magento was purchased again, this time by Adobe. So in addition to the main website at https://magento.com, you can also find the official Adobe page for Magento at https://adobe.com/commerce/magento.html.

## WHAT DOES MAGENTO MEAN?

There are two different stories about the origin of the Magento name.

In one story, Magento was originally called Bento, but legal issues meant that they couldn't use that name. So, the team decided to add the word "Mage", a Dungeons and Dragons-style wizard. "Bento" became "Magento".

In the other story, the name Magento was derived from the color magenta. The two founders of Magento, Roy and Yoav, wanted a magenta-colored logo, partly because the Varien logo was also purple. However, because the domain magenta.com had already been registered, the team looked at variations on that word and ended up choosing "Magento".

Apologies to those of you reading in black-and-white, but the image below shows the first version of the Magento logo, which was a magenta color:

Soon, the Magento logo was using orange instead, and it remains that way today:

MAGENTO 1 OR MAGENTO 2?

In this book, you use Magento 2, which is the latest and greatest version.

There are two major, and very different, versions of Magento:

- **Magento 1** was released in 2008. Some websites still use it. However, with the release of Magento 2, support for Magento 1 is now limited.

- **Magento 2** was released in 2015 with significant improvements to Magento's code and user interface.

Magento 1 and Magento 2 are very different software, so it is difficult to move between these two versions. I always recommend that you build new sites with Magento 2.

## MAGENTO COMMERCE OR MAGENTO OPEN SOURCE?

In this book, we use Magento Open Source.

We mentioned earlier that there has been a commercial option called "Magento Enterprise " since 2009. That product is now called "Magento Commerce", and you need to pay to use it.

The free option was called "Magento Community Edition" and is now called "Magento Open Source". This software is 100% free to download and use.

## WHY SHOULD YOU CHOOSE MAGENTO?

- **Magento is powerful.** Magento provides you with many ready-built features. If you want a new site design, or wish to add a calendar, or shopping cart to your site, you can often do it with just a few clicks. It may take a few days or even weeks to build a great Magento site, but you can develop and launch more quickly than with many alternatives.

- **Magento is cheaper.** Building a Magento site is unlikely to be completely cost-free. You may have purchased this book or other training, and you might need to hire an expert. A good Magento site can cost between a few dollars and hundreds of thousands of dollars. However, it costs you nothing to get into Magento, whereas commercial alternatives to Magento often cost hundreds of thousands of dollars before you even start.

- **Magento has more options.** If you'd like extra features on your Magento site, https://marketplace.magento.com has hundreds of ready-to-use extensions and themes available. You can do many things with Magento without writing a line of code. However, you may have to hire a developer if you have unusual or specific requirements.

## WHO USES MAGENTO?

Everyone from tech powerhouses to corporations that span the world use Magento to power their web presence. And, let's not forget the non-profits that support the people. The list goes on and on. Below are just a few examples we hope will inspire you.

**Tech**: Magento powers the online stores for many technology companies. Vizio makes consumer electronics and are particularly well-known for their televisions. Their website at http://vizio.com is built in Magento. Other tech companies using Magento include 20th Century Fox at https://foxconnect.com and Olympus at http://getolympus.com.

**Sports and Health**: Magento has carved out a niche in the fitness world. Body&Fit is a company from the Netherlands whose Dutch-language site is at https://bodyenfitshop.nl. Adidas and Nike have used Magento, and so have sports teams such as the Atlanta Hawks https://hawksshop.com and Liverpool http://store.liverpoolfc.com.

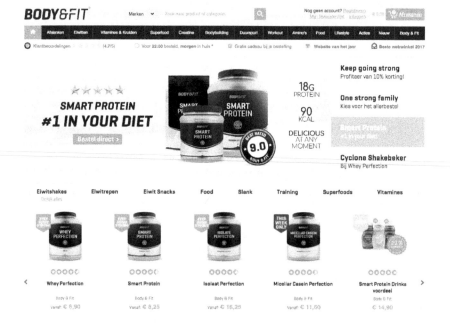

**Business**: Many successful organizations around the world use Magento. Two famous companies that use Magento for consumer-facing sites are Ford at https://accessories.ford.com and Land Rover at https://shop.landrover.com. General Motors uses Magento for a very large internal platform for its dealers.

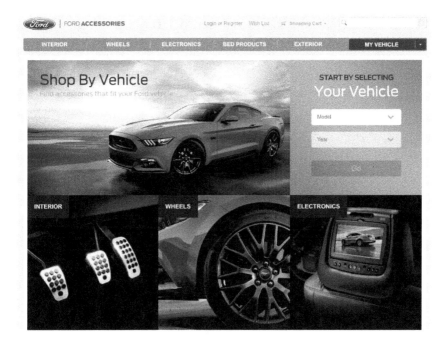

**Consumer Products**: Companies don't get any more high-profile than Coca-Cola. If you want to buy Coke-branded products, visit https://buy.shareacoke.com. If you prefer something a little stronger, try http://store.jackdaniels.co.uk.

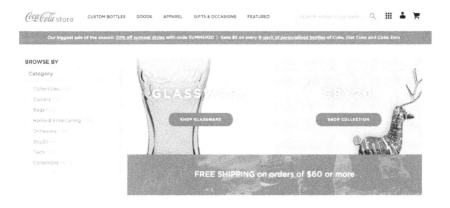

**Fashion**: When looking for famous Magento stores, fashion was the biggest category I came across. Eileen Fisher's Magento site at https://eileenfisher.com/shop is shown in the image below . You can also check out Helly Hansen at https://hellyhansen.com,

Oscar De La Renta at http://oscardelarenta.com and Spanx at http://spanx.com.

**Non-profits**: Magento is used by many charities and non-profit organizations to increase their revenues. The image below shows the Magento-powered website for the Royal Academy of the Arts in London at  https://shop.royalacademy.org.uk . Also check out the American Museum of Natural History in New York at https://shop.amnh.org.

You can see a more detailed list of sites built with Magento at https://magento.com/customers.

WHAT'S NEXT?

In this chapter, you learned important information about Magento.

The next step is to set up your Magento site so that you have a platform to build on.

Are you ready? If you are, turn to the next chapter, and let's begin.

# GETTING SET UP FOR THIS BOOK

This book is almost entirely hands-on. Throughout the remaining chapters, we're going to build a store called "Orangeville". We're going to fill this store with products in Magento-orange.

So, in order to follow the steps in this book, you will need a Magento website. Please don't use your company's live site for the exercises in this book!

Read through this chapter, and we'll give you advice on how to set up a new, clean Magento site where you are free to experiment and learn.

## YOUR GOAL AT THE START OF THIS BOOK

Ideally, when you start this book, you will have a new Magento site with no sample data. A new Magento site will look like this image below.

Once you get a new Magento site that looks like the image above, make sure to bookmark the URL in your browser.

I'd also recommend bookmarking the admin login screen for your new Magento site, shown in the image below.

Book marking the admin login URL is important because not every Magento site has the same URL for the admin area.

With most platforms, the admin URL never changes. For example, with WordPress, the admin URL is always example.com/wp-admin/. With Joomla, the admin URL is always example.com/administrator/

However, with Magento, your admin URL can be different for each site. This is a security measure so that hackers can't easily find your admin URL. But, it does make it easy to forget your URL. I move between different Magento sites, I often forget the location of the admin area is on each site and have to look at my bookmarks.

OK, so now you know what we're looking for in order to start the book.

Your next question is probably "How do I get a site like that?"

Let's look at options for where you install a new Magento Site.

### WHERE TO HOST YOUR MAGENTO SITE

Magento is not like many other software programs. It can't just run on any computer. It requires a server to run successfully. That means you normally have the choice of installing Magento in one of three places:

1. A local server
2. A web server
3. A web server maintained by Magento experts

Choosing the best place to install Magento is important, so here is an explanation of the difference between the three options.

**Important**: Magento can be slow. I would go so far as to say that Magento is famous for being slow. Generally this is because people install it on servers that do not have enough power to run a Magento site. If you use Magento on an ordinary server and then on a different server which has been optimized for Magento, you will notice a significant difference in speed.

## MAGENTO HOSTING OPTION #1. A LOCAL SERVER

We do not recommend that beginners use a local server installed on your computer.

It can be tempting to choose this route. More advanced users find several useful advantages to working on your computer:

- **Working offline:** You can work without an Internet connection.

- **Privacy:** Your Magento site will be safe and private, accessible only to people who can access that computer.

- **Free:** There are no fees to pay.

However, there are also several important disadvantages to using a computer:

- **Extra installations needed:** You need to download and configure special software for your computer.

- **Difficult to get help:** You can't easily show it to other people and ask for help.

- **Only on one computer:** You can access it only from the computer you used to install it.

- **Need to move to launch:** When you're ready to make your site public, you need to move everything to a web server and adjust for any differences between the two locations.

Because of these disadvantages, installing on your computer can present significant obstacles for a beginner. Do not take this route until you have more experience.

If you do want to install Magento on your local server, check out the instructions at http://ostraining.com/books/magento/local.

## MAGENTO HOSTING OPTION #2. A WEB SERVER

Unlike your computer, a web server is specifically designed for hosting websites so that they are easy to visit for anyone who's online.

If you work for a company, it might provide a server. However, many people need to rent space from a hosting company.

Your server will need to run PHP and MySQL. The need for PHP is because Magento is written in it, and you need MySQL because it is the type of database Magento normally uses. These are the minimum versions needed:

- **PHP:** 5.6 or above

- **MySQL:** 5.6 or above

Magento runs best on an Apache or Ngnix server. It is also possible to run Magento on a Windows server.

If you do want to install Magento on a web server, check out the instructions at http://ostraining.com/books/magento/web.

## MAGENTO HOSTING OPTION #3. A WEB SERVER MAINTAINED BY MAGENTO EXPERTS

You can install Magento on almost any server that has PHP and MySQL installed. However, Magento is a large platform and many hosting companies struggle to run it correctly. I recommend you choose a hosting company that specializes in Magento.

We recommend https://nexcess.net as a Magento host, and that's who we will be using for examples in this book.

There are at least five important advantages to choosing a Magento-specific hosting service, such as Nexcess:

1. **Ease-of-installation**. Good hosts will often install Magento for you automatically, as soon as you sign up. With Nexcess, as you're signing up, they'll ask if you want to use Magento. If you say "Yes", they will automatically install Magento for you. Your Magento site will be ready to use as soon as you log in.
2. **Support.** You don't want your hosting company to offer support only 9 am to 5pm. Your site could go down at any tine. Nexcess has 24/7 phone and email support. Their team knows what they're doing.
3. **Expertise**. Many hosts only have a few Magento sites. Nexcess hosts over 40,000 Magento sites and are an official Magento Technology Partner. They know Magento.
4. **Servers**. It's not easy to run an e-commerce server, and this is particularly true for Magento, which has some quirky requirements. You need servers that are managed by Magento experts who know exactly what Magento sites need to run well.
5. **Cron jobs**. Magento sites need to have cron jobs set up in order to run correctly. Nexcess has cron jobs set up and correctly configured for you.

Here's how you can get started with a site hosted at Nexcess:

- Go to http://nexcess.net and click the "Cloud" logo:

- Click one of the green "SIGN UP" buttons.

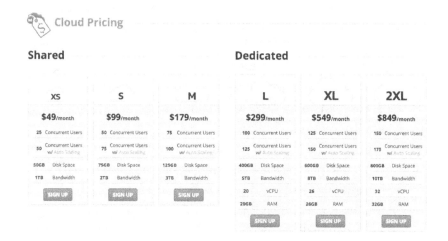

- Create an account using your email address and a password:

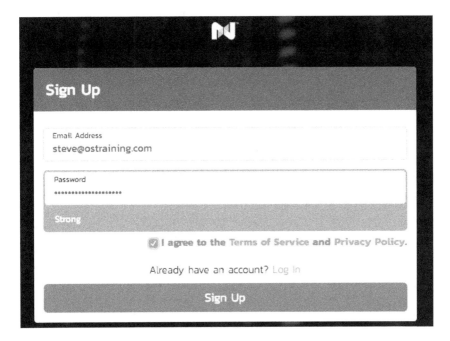

- Choose a domain name for your website. It is highly likely that you will NOT need to use this domain name while working on this book. You will get a temporary domain name that you can use while building your site. The normal process when building a site is to use a temporary URL and then only use your real domain name when the site is ready to go live.

- Click "Next" to proceed.

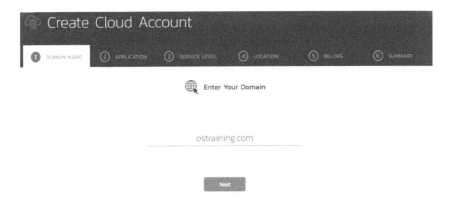

- Choose Magento from the different platforms on offer.

- Select "Yes" for the choice at the bottom next to the text that says "You selected an app environment optimized for Magento. Would you also like us to automatically install Magento for you into this environment?"

- Click "Next" to proceed.

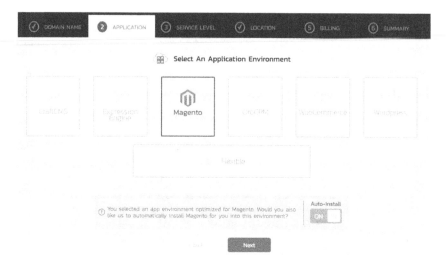

- Choose the level of resources you need. When you're learning or launching your site, you should have no problem using the smallest of these plans.

- Click "Next" to proceed.

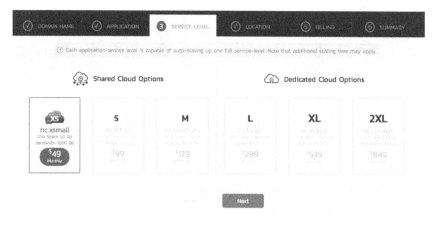

- Enter your billing details.

- Check that the summary of your sign-up details is correct.

- Click "Create Account".

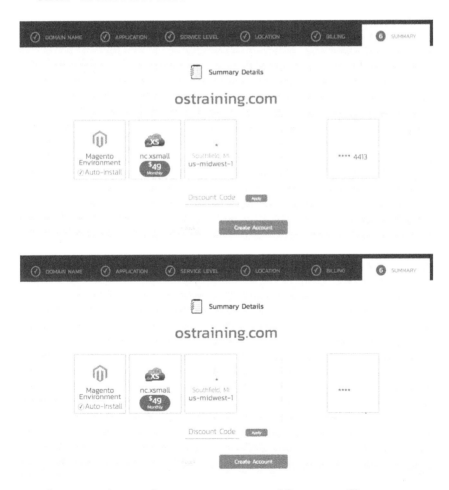

- After completing the sign-up process, Nexcess will

automatically install your Magento site. The installation process may take a few minutes.

- When your site is ready, you'll see all the details of your app. There will be a temporary URL you can use to access your site. With Nexcess, the temporary URL is often a string of numbers and letters, as you can see in the image below.

- If you click on your temporary domain name, you will now see your new Magento site:

The final step in this setup process is to get the username and password for your site.

- Look inside your Nexcess dashboard, and click the blue menu on the right side of the screen.

- Click "Control Panel" from the dropdown links.

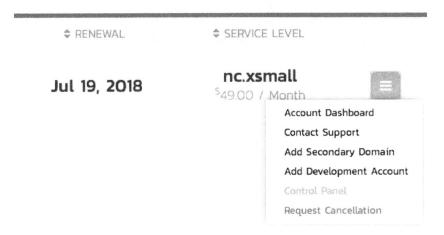

- Under the "Environment" tab of your Control Panel, you can access the username and password for your site.

- Click the blue "App Admin" button in the image above.

- You'll see the Magento admin screen in the image below. Enter the username and password that you just found and you'll be granted access to your new Magento site.

However, I do have one final piece of advice before you dive into the rest of the book and start building your Magento site.

A good website builder never practices on their live site. You don't want to test out your changes on a site where customers can see your changes. So Nexcess provides you with an easy way to create a test version of your site where you can happily make all the changes you want. Plus if you break anything, you can always create a new test site.

Follow the instructions here: https://ostra.in/dev-sites. Nexcess will create an exact copy of your Magento site with the same username and password. you will even be able to access the development site from the same place in your control panel, as shown in the image below.

## GETTING HELP WITH INSTALLATIONS

There are three places you should go to for help if you get stuck while installing Magento.

1.  **The Magento Forum:** It's almost guaranteed that someone has experienced the same Magento installation problem as you and has asked about it on http://ostra.in/magento-install. It's a great place to search for solutions and ask for help.
2.  **The Magento documentation:** There's an official installation guide at http://ostra.in/magento-docs.
3.  **Magento 2 Explained:** https://ostraining.com/books/magento/ has video tutorials, written tutorials and links to help with your installation. You can also email us via books@ostraining.com.

## WHAT'S NEXT?

You now have a Magento site ready to use. In the next chapter, you tour your new site and are introduced to the most important things you need to know.

Are you ready?

Turn the page and let's start learning Magento.

# YOUR FIRST 12 MAGENTO TASKS

In this chapter, we're going to take a quick tour of your Magento site.

The goal is not only to get you familiar with Magento's user interface, but also to introduce you to some key Magento features that you'll be using throughout this book.

We're not going to dive deep into any particular feature at this time, but we will start to make some changes to your store.

We have 12 small tasks that will help you feel more comfortable with Magento:

1. Change your account details
2. Understand the Sales pages
3. Create your first product
4. Create a customer
5. Change the welcome email
6. Create a discount coupon
7. Change the homepage
8. Change the logo
9. Change the store name
10. Set the store details
11. Buy a product
12. Disable the cache

At the start of this chapter, your site should look like the image below. By the end of this chapter, you will have a working store!

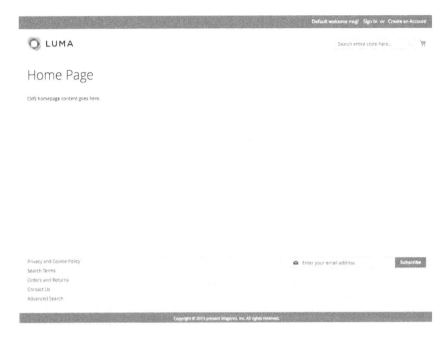

## TASK #1. CHANGE YOUR ACCOUNT DETAILS

At the end of the chapter "Magento Installations Explained", you installed your new Magento site and logged in. Congratulations! You're now ready to explore your Magento site.

On the left of the site, you now see a vertical administration menu, starting with "Dashboard" and "Sales", then dropping down to "System" and "Find Partners & Extensions". This menu is the most important part of your site. Almost everything you want to change and modify on your site can be accessed from here.

The links in this menu are organized according to how often they're used. When you're using Magento, you'll spend most of your time using the top links, such as "Sales", "Catalog", "Customers", and "Marketing".

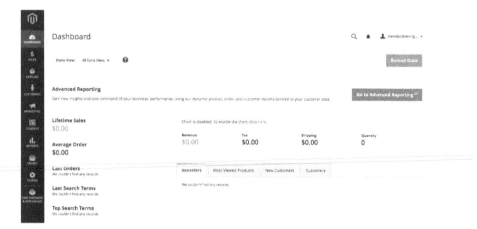

In the top-right corner of the screen, you'll see a search box. This is a quick way to find information in your store. This won't help you find different features of your store (you can't search for a particular configuration option), but it will search for products, orders, customers and content pages.

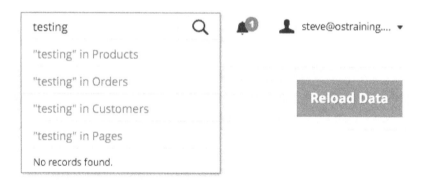

Next to the search box, you'll find an alert box. It may be empty at the moment, but this is one way that the Magento team keeps you up-to-date with important news. For example, in this image below, the Magento team has just released version 2.2.

Next to the search box and alert box, there's also a dropdown menu.

- "Account Setting" will allow you to edit your username and password.
- "Customer View" will send you directly to the front of the site.
- "Sign Out" will log you out and send you to the front of the site.

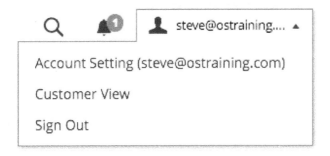

Let's try one of those links. Let's make sure that our account details are correct.

- Click on "Account Setting".
- Update your account. Most likely your "First Name" and "Last Name" fields are not correct.

- To save changes, you will need to re-enter your password in the "Your Password" area at the bottom of the screen.
- Click "Save Account".

## Account Information

| | |
|---|---|
| User Name * | steve@ostraining.com |
| First Name * | Steve |
| Last Name * | Burge |
| Email * | steve@ostraining.com |
| New Password | |
| Password Confirmation | |
| Interface Locale | English (United States) / English (United States) ▾ |

## Current User Identity Verification

| | |
|---|---|
| Your Password * | •••••••••• |
| | This is a required field. |

## TASK #2. UNDERSTAND THE SALES PAGES

Now that we know what options are available via the "Dashboard" link, let's move on to the "Sales" link. This menu has seven sub-menu links:

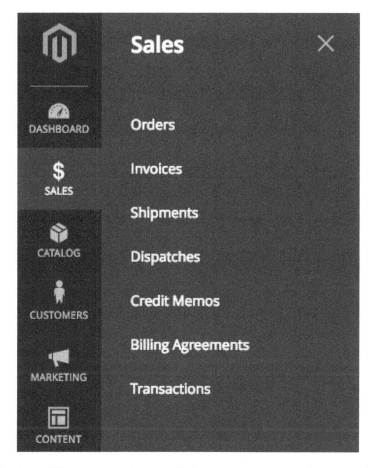

- Orders: This screen shows all the attempts users have made to buy products from your site.

- Invoices: This screen shows finalized invoices. Lots of orders never end up in an invoice. The reason for this is because they might have been abandoned before an invoice was created.

- Shipments: This screen shows details of any outbound shipments, including how the product was shipped, when it was shipped, and who it was shipped to.

- Dispatches: This screens gives information about products that have shipped to customers.

- Credit Memos: This screen lists money that is returned to customers. This could be a refund for missing or damaged goods. Or, it could be that the customer forgot to enter a discount code they wanted to use.

- Billing Agreements: This shows customer payment details that have been saved to the site. Customers who return to make multiple purchases don't have to re-enter their payment details each time.

- Transactions: This screen lists all payment activity that has taken place between your store and external payment systems.

Many of these seven different areas are closely tied together.

For example, when a customer successfully creates an "Order", it will generate listings in "Invoices" and "Transactions". If the customer chooses to save their payment details, there will also be a listing in "Billing Agreements". Finally, when the product is sent out, another listing will appear in "Shipments".

To give another example, when you refund an "Order", it may generate a listing in "Credit Memos" and also "Transactions".

Not only are the "Sales" areas closely related, but they all share a very similar layout. Let's take a look at one of these areas. Once you're comfortable with one area, it will be easy to navigate all the others.

- Click on the "Orders" link.

- You can now see the main Orders screen, showing all the orders received by your store.

Your site doesn't have any orders yet, but this next image shows how this screen looks with some sample orders:

Across the top of the screen, you can use several tools to find particular orders.

There's a search box for orders, although this is just a more focused version of the search box we saw earlier:

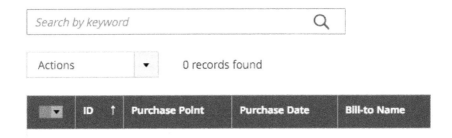

There's a "Filters" option that allows you to drill down according to multiple criteria, including the date, status and cost of the order:

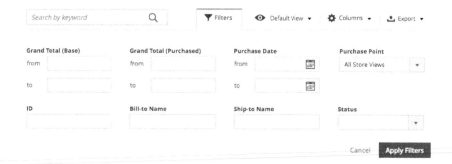

You can use the "Columns" option to choose the details shown on this screen:

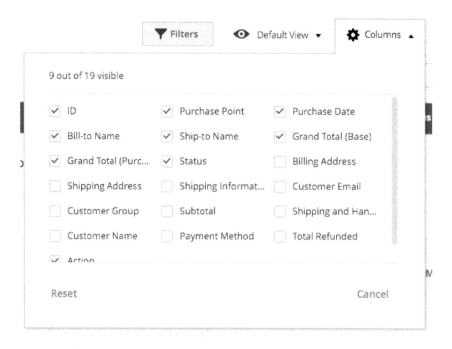

Finally, when you do have orders, you can perform bulk actions on them, using the dropdown menu on the left:

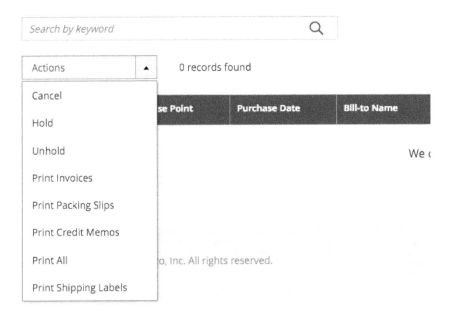

All of the pages you'll see on your Magento site share a very similar layout. We've just seen the "Orders" screen. Let's compare that to the "Invoices" screen, which is the next link under "Sales". These screens can be divided into four areas. Everywhere you go inside Magento, you'll see this same layout:

1. Page Title
2. Internal search and important links
3. Filters and actions
4. Table with key information

This next image shows the same layout for the "Credit Memos" page:

## TASK #3. CREATE YOUR FIRST PRODUCT

Some of Magento's admin areas are complex. The "Reports" and "System" areas both have at least 15 different options.

Some admin areas are much simpler: "Products" has just two links:

- Catalog: This is a list of all your products.
- Categories: This is a list of how you're organizing your products.

Let's add your first product to the Orangeville store.

- In the Magento admin area, go to "Catalog", and then "Products".

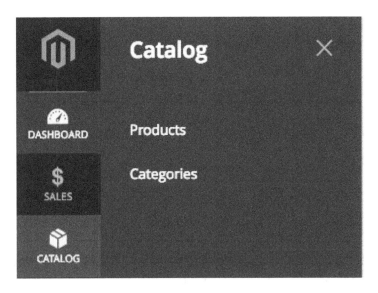

You now see the main Products page, which contains a list of all the products on your site. Right now, this list is absolutely empty. Let's fix that.

- Click the big, orange, "Add Product" button in the top-right corner:

You now see the "New Product" screen. Let's enter the details for our first product. Of course, we're going to create an orange product!

- Product Name: **Carrots**

- SKU: **FOOD101.** This is an abbreviation of "Stock Keeping Unit", and is a unique code for this product.

- Price: **1.00**

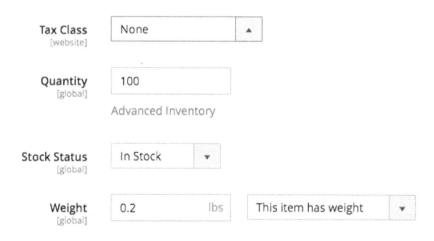

| | |
|---|---|
| Enable Product [website] | ( ) Yes |
| Attribute Set | Default ▾ |
| Product Name * [store view] | Carrots |
| SKU * [global] | FOOD101 |
| Price * [global] | $ 1.00 |

Scrolling a little further down the page, let's enter some more information for our new product:

- Tax Class: **None**
- Quantity: **100**
- Stock Status: **In Stock**
- Weight: **0.2 lbs**

| | |
|---|---|
| Tax Class [website] | None ▲ |
| Quantity [global] | 100 |
| | Advanced Inventory |
| Stock Status [global] | In Stock ▾ |
| Weight [global] | 0.2 lbs | This item has weight ▾ |

So far, so good. Now we can come to the Categories area, where we can organize our products.

- Click on the "Select" dropdown.

- You'll see there's one option: "Default Category". Check this box and click "Done".

Scroll down the page, and you'll see a larger area with lots of sliders. These sliders hide many more possibilities for our product.

- Click on the "Images and Videos" slider.

- You'll see a box that says "Browse to find or drag image here".

- If you haven't done so yet, download the files from http://ostraining.com/books/magento. These are the images and resources you can use to follow on as we build the Orangeville store.

- Click on "Browse to find or drag image here".

- Look in the files you downloaded, open the "vegetables" folder, and choose the file called carrots.jpg.

- You will now see that the image has been successfully uploaded:

## Images And Videos

960x487 px, 853 KB

Base   Small   Swatch

Thumbnail

That's it. That's all we're going to do for our first product. Let's save our changes.

- Click "Save & Close" in the top-right corner.

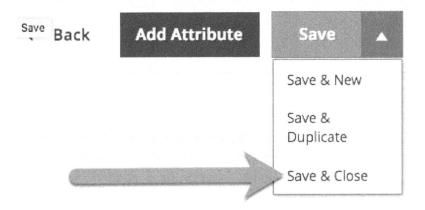

You'll now go back to the main Products page. You'll see your new product, plus a message that says "You saved the product."

Congratulations! You've created your first Magento product!

There's only one problem.

The product is nowhere to be seen on your site.

Go to your store's homepage, and you'll see the same blank area as before. A little later, in Step #7, we'll show this product on our homepage.

## TASK #4. CREATE A NEW CUSTOMER

If the "Products" area was simple, the "Customers" area is equally simple. There just two links:

- All Customers: A list of every customer registered in your store.

- Now Online: A list of customers who logged in most recently.

- Customer Groups: You can divide up your customers and give different benefits to different groups.

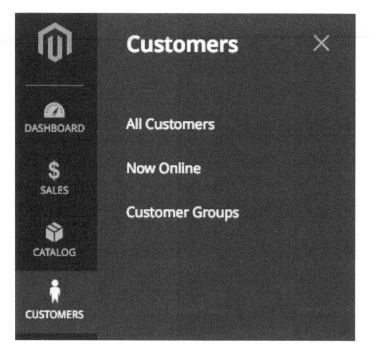

- Click on the "All Customers" tab. You'll see a screen that follows exactly the same format as the "Sales" and "Products" pages.

- Click the "Add New Customer" button.

- Let's create a new customer that we can use to test our products. Enter the "First Name", "Last Name", and "Email" fields.

## Account Information

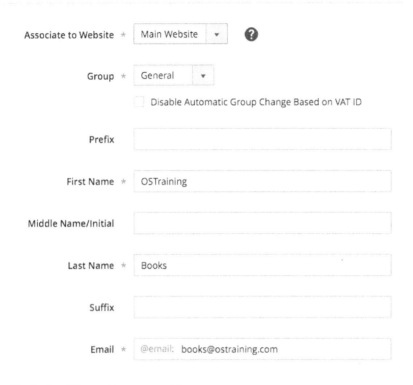

- Click the "Save Customer" button.
- Check the inbox for the email address you just entered. Hopefully, you received a welcome email that looks like the image below.

**Welcome to Main Website Store**    Inbox   x                                    🖶 ▣

**Owner** owner@example.com <u>via</u> managedcloudhostingemail.com          12:02 PM (3 minutes ago)    ⤺   ▾
to OSTraining  ▾

OSTraining Books,

Welcome to Main Website Store.

To sign in to our site and set a password, click on the link:

- **Email:** books@ostraining.com

When you sign in to your account, you will be able to:

- Proceed through checkout faster
- Check the status of orders
- View past orders
- Store alternative addresses (for shipping to multiple family members and friends)

About Us
Customer Service

If you didn't receive the email, don't worry. Receiving the email is not essential for following along with this book. It could be because you have Magento installed on your computer (where email is often disabled) or on a hosting company where more steps are needed to configure email sending.

Did you notice that several things are very generic about this email? These two items are especially obvious:

- There's a default logo: LUMA
- There's a default site name: "Main Website Store".

We're going to fix those items later in this chapter.

- If you did get this welcome email: click on the "link" text in the email.
- You will be taken to the screen below to set a password for

your new customer account. Create a password for your account and save it. We'll be using that account later in this chapter.

# Set a New Password

New Password *

Password Strength: No Password

Confirm New Password *

**Set a New Password**

## TASK #5. CUSTOMIZE THE WELCOME EMAIL

The previous two areas, "Products" and "Customers", only had two links.

In contract, the "Marketing" menu area has 14 links spread across six different groups:

- Promotions: You can give discounts on specific products or for specific users.

- Communications: You can send newsletters to your customers.

- Social: This allows you to set up a Facebook store with products from your Magento site.

- SEO & Search: You can optimize your site for search engines using site maps and other Google-friendly features.

- User Content: This feature allows users to leave reviews on your products.

- Marketing Automation: This is a paid upgrade that allows you to send targeted emails to customers.

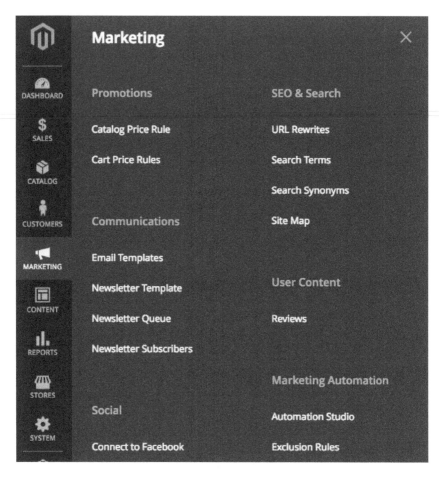

Let's take a look at "Communications". This area of Magento enables you to customize and send emails to customers. We're going to edit the welcome email that we just saw earlier in the chapter.

- Click "Marketing", and then "Email Templates":

- Click the orange "Add New Template" button in the top-right of the screen.

- From the "Template" dropdown, choose "New Account Without Password".

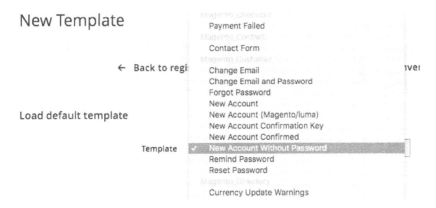

- Click the "Load Template" button:

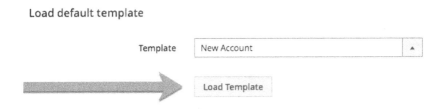

- You'll now see that the email boxes are filled in. This is the welcome email that we saw earlier in the chapter. All users receive this when they register on your site. You can edit this text and write your own welcome message for new customers.

- Template Name: **Our customized Orangeville new account email**
- In the main text, replace "To sign in to our site" with "To sign in to the Orangeville site".

- Click the "Save Template" button when you're done.
- Click the "Preview" button.

- You'll now see a pop-up window with a preview of the Welcome email. It looks very similar to the email you received. It is missing our personal information, but in all other ways, it's identical … except for our small change.

These Email Templates are sent automatically when specific situations occur on your site. Inside the "Communications" area, you'll also find options for sending newsletters. These are marketing newsletters you can send whenever you want. These can be important, and we'll deal with newsletters in more detail later in the chapter "Magento Marketing Explained".

## TASK #6. CREATE A DISCOUNT

Let's stay in the "Marketing" area for the next task. Under the "Promotions" header, you'll see two options for Promotions,

"Catalog Price Rules" and "Cart Price Rules". In Magento, "Promotions" refers to discounts and coupon codes.

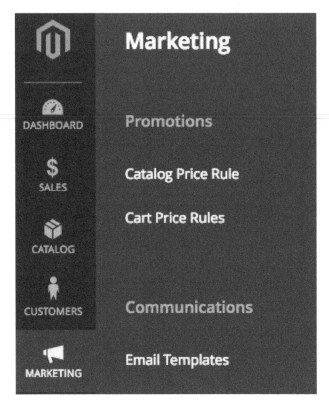

"Catalog Price Rules" are discounts that are applied to the products before they go in the shopping cart. In the example below, 20% is taken off all women's and men's pants. The customer doesn't have to do anything to get this discount. They don't need to have a coupon code or spend a specific amount of money.

"Cart Price Rules" are best described as discounts that are applied in the shopping cart. These discounts are applied automatically when the customer enters a valid coupon code, or has met other conditions.

- Save 70% with the coupon code "orange70".

- Buy 3 shirts and get the 4th free.

- Spend over $50 and shipping is free.

- 20% off purchases over $200.

In all these situations, the customer has to enter a coupon, spend a certain amount of money, or buy a specific quantity of products.

In this task, we're going to create a coupon in "Cart Price Rules".

- Click "Marketing", and then "Cart Price Rules".

- Click "Add New Rule".

- Rule Name: **Orange Discount**

- Description: **This is a 20% discount for everyone who likes the color orange**

- Active: Yes

- Websites: Main Website

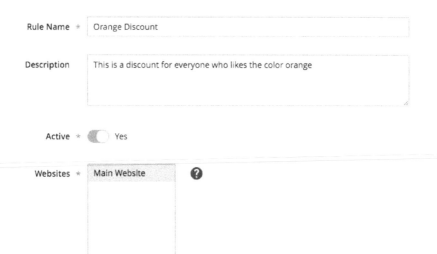

- Customer Groups: **General**
- Coupon: **Specific Coupon**
- Coupon Code: **orange20**

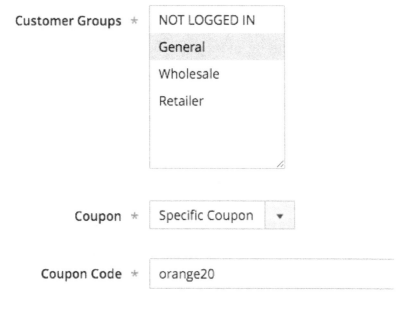

- Click the "Actions" tab.

- Apply: **Precent of product price discount**
- Discount Amount: **20**

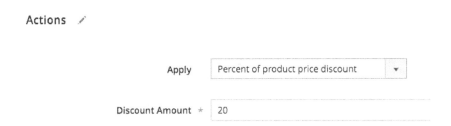

## TASK #7. CHANGE THE HOMEPAGE

The "Content" area of your site contains almost everything that is not directly related to Products. We're going to use the "Pages" and "Widgets" features to update our homepage.

- Click on the "Pages" link:

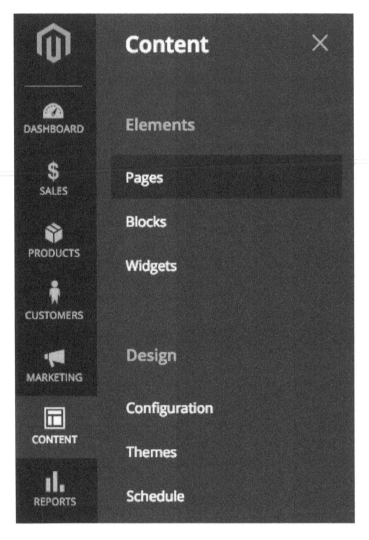

You'll now see a list of content pages on your site. There are four pages already created:

- 404 Not Found: This can be found if you type a broken URL.

- Home page: This controls the blank frontpage we've seen so far.

- Enable Cookies:This text asks visitors to enable cookies if they have them disabled in their browser.

- Privacy and Cookie Policy: This link is also in the footer menu of your site.

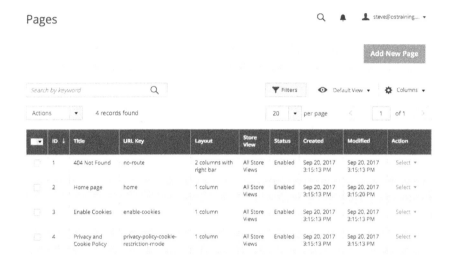

Let's edit the homepage and change the text that visitors see.

- In the "Home page" row, click "Select" and then "Edit".

- You'll now see the screen that controls your site's homepage.
- Click on the "Content" tab:

- When the "Content" tab opens, you'll see the "CMS homepage content goes here." text.

- Edit the "Content Heading" field so that it says "The Orangeville Homepage".

- Edit the text so that it says "**Welcome to Orangeville! This store is perfect for everyone who loves orange!**"

Content  ✐

Content Heading       The Orangeville Homepage

Welcome to Orangeville! This store is perfect for everyone who loves orange!

Now we're going to insert a Magento feature that will show all your products. Magento calls this feature a "Widget".

- Place your cursor into the main text area, below the two sentences you've just written.

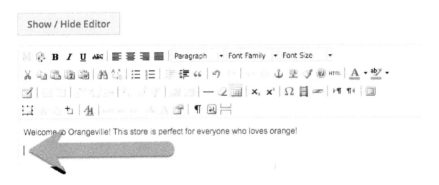

- Click the small Magento icon on the top-left corner of the text editor:

- Choose "Catalog Products List" from the "Widget Type" dropdown.

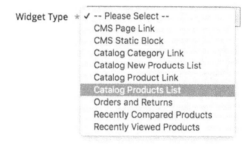

- Skip all of the options and click the orange "Insert Widget" button, which is in the bottom-right corner:

- An orange box now appears in the editor area. The box has "New" over the icon and "products" next to the icon.

- Click the "Save Page" button in the top-right corner.
- In the top-right corner, click "Customer View":

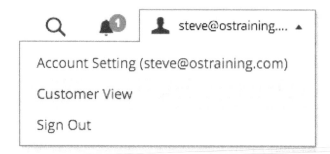

- You'll now see that your homepage has the updated text and is showing your first product!

This is a very typical example of the changes you can make in the "Content" area of your site. We're going to come back here often, including in the next chapter when we'll make further changes to our homepage.

### TASK #8. CHANGE THE LOGO

Now what we've added our first product and changed the content of our homepage, let's make a design change as well. We're going to replace the "Luma" logo with an Orangeville logo.

- Click on "Configuration":

- Click "Edit" in the top row:

This page has all the settings for your store's design. Here you can change many design settings, including your store's logo, favicon, and footer text.

- Scroll down and click the "Header" area:

- Upload the orangeville-logo.png file from your Magento resources folder:

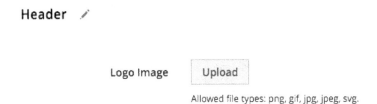

- Here's how the option will appear after you've selected the image:

**Header** 🖉

Logo Image    Upload    ↰ Use Default Value

Allowed file types: png, gif, jpg, jpeg, svg.

78x457, 3 KB

- Click the "Save Configuration" button.
- Visit the front of your site, and you'll see the new logo:

Orangeville

## The Orangeville Homepage

Welcome to Orangeville! This store is perfect for everyone who loves orange!

## TASK #9. CHANGE THE STORE NAME

We've now been into most of the menu areas in Magento, but we haven't been into "Stores" yet.

You might be a little confused and ask yourself "Why does Magento use the word 'Stores' when I only have one store"?

The answer is that it is possible to run multiple stores from a single site. By default, this option isn't set up, but it is one of the more advanced options that attracts people to Magento. You could also have "Purpleville", "Yellowville" and "Blueville" running from this same dashboard. In this book, we're not going talk about creating multiple stores with one Magento site. It's a complex subject and requires some coding setup. But if you want to learn more about this "Stores" feature, visit https://ostra.in/stores.

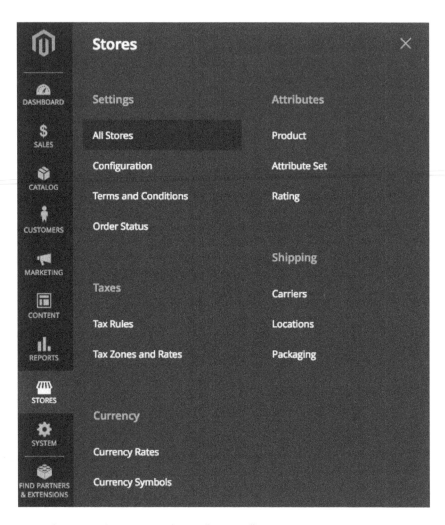

Our first exploration of the "Stores" area will be to change the name of our store.

- Click "Stores", and then "All Stores".
- Click "Main Website Store".

- Name: **Orangeville Store**
- Click "Save Store".

This should ensure that "Orangeville Store" is now used to refer to your site instead of "Main Website Store".

Store Information

## TASK #10. SET YOUR STORE DETAILS

Also inside the "Stores" area, we can set the address and other key details for our store.

- Click "Stores", and then "Configuration".

In this area you can tell Magento more about your store.

- Click "Country Options", and you can choose which country your store is based in:

Country Options

- Click "Locale Options", and you can choose your timezone, language and measurement units:

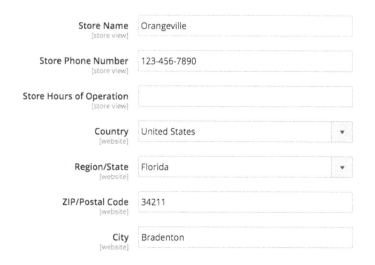

- Click "Store Information" and enter in the address for your store:

**Store Information**

| | |
|---|---|
| **Store Name** [store view] | Orangeville |
| **Store Phone Number** [store view] | 123-456-7890 |
| **Store Hours of Operation** [store view] | |
| **Country** [website] | United States |
| **Region/State** [website] | Florida |
| **ZIP/Postal Code** [website] | 34211 |
| **City** [website] | Bradenton |

## TASK #11. BUY YOUR FIRST PRODUCT

Now, let's put together all the new skills we've learned from doing these tasks. Let's make our first Magento purchase.

- Go to the front of your site.
- Click the "Sign In" link and log in using the customer account you created in task #4. Magento doesn't allow you to log in as a customer using your admin account.

- After you have logged in, you'll be taken to an account page:

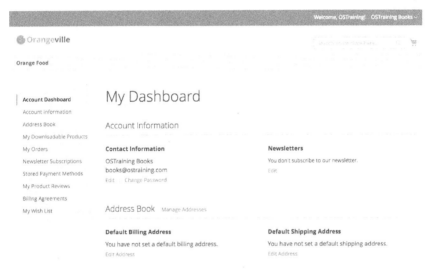

- Go back to the homepage.
- Click the "Add to Cart" button for the carrots.

 Orangeville

# The Orangeville Homepage

Welcome to Orangeville! This store is perfect for everyone who loves orange!

Carrots

**$1.00**

- In the top-right corner of the site, click the cart icon. You'll see a pop-up with your cart details.
- Click the blue "Go to Checkout" button.

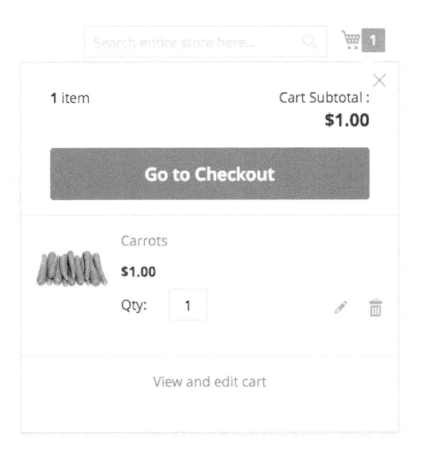

- On the checkout page, you will be asked for an address and phone number:

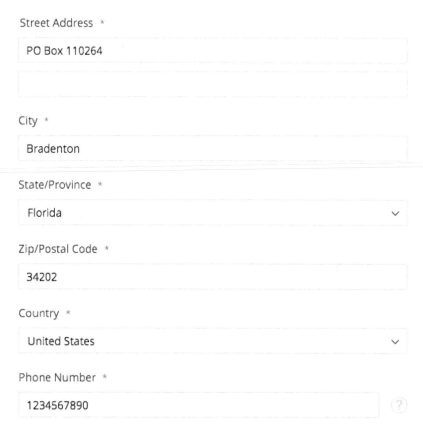

Street Address *

PO Box 110264

City *

Bradenton

State/Province *

Florida ⌄

Zip/Postal Code *

34202

Country *

United States ⌄

Phone Number *

1234567890 ⑦

- Click the blue "Next" button by "Shipping Methods" at the bottom of the page. Yes, $5 seems a lot to ship one single carrot. We'll have to fix that later in the book.

Shipping Methods

○ $5.00        Fixed        Flat Rate

Next

- On the next page, you'll see the final checkout details.
- In the "Apply Discount Code" area, enter "orange20".
- Click "Apply Discount", and you'll save 20% on the price of

your carrot. This saves you 20 cents! Unfortunately, you still have to pay the whole price of the shipping.

- Click the blue "Place Order" button.

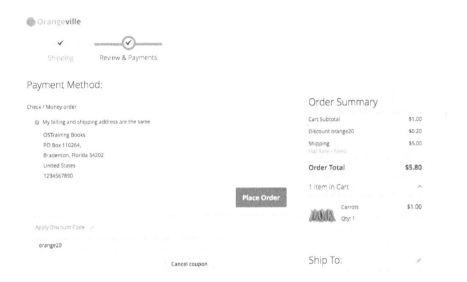

Congratulations! You've made your first Magento purchase of your first Magento product on your first Magento store!

You don't have to pay anything yet because we haven't set up a payment gateway yet. We'll talk about payment options later in the book.

If your site is successfully sending email, you should receive an email to confirm the order.

- Let's go back into our site's admin area.

- Click "Sales", and then "Orders". You'll see your order is marked as "Pending":

| | ID ↑ | Purchase Point | Purchase Date | Bill-to Name | Ship-to Name | Grand Total (Base) | Grand Total (Purchased) | Status | Action |
|---|---|---|---|---|---|---|---|---|---|
| ☐ | 000000001 | Main Website Orangeville Store Default Store View | Oct 04, 2017, 12:10:00 PM | OSTraining Books | OSTraining Books | $5.80 | $5.80 | Pending | View |

However, notice that there are no entries in "Invoices" or "Transactions" yet. As we add billing and shipping options to our Magento store, we'll see how one order can automatically trigger those other Sales features.

## TASK #12. DISABLE THE CACHE

We're nearly at the end of this chapter, and we've been into almost every section of the Magento admin area, except for "System". This menu link contains all sorts of technical options for running our site. Here we can make backups, control user permissions, import /export data and do much more.

What we're going to do in this chapter is turn off the cache. The cache will save copies of our pages, so that they load more quickly. That's a good thing when our site is complete, but not when we're learning and making frequent changes. Have you noticed that any of your changes in this chapter have taken a few moments to show? The cache is probably the reason why.

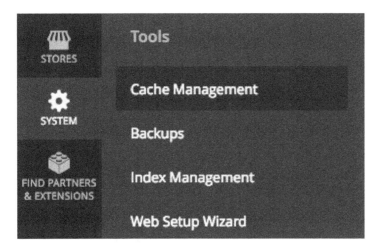

- Go to "System", and then "Cache Management".
- Select all of the cache types using the checkboxes on the left side of the screen:

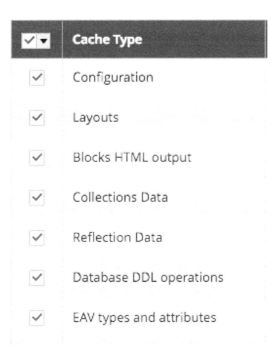

- Choose "Disable" in the dropdown box.
- Click "Submit".

- When you're finished, all the caches should have a red "DISABLED" box next to them. This will make it much faster for you to see any future changes you make during this book.

| Cache Type | Description | Tags | Status |
|---|---|---|---|
| Configuration | Various XML configurations that were collected across modules and merged | CONFIG | DISABLED |
| Layouts | Layout building instructions | LAYOUT_GENERAL_CACHE_TAG | DISABLED |
| Blocks HTML output | Page blocks HTML | BLOCK_HTML | DISABLED |
| Collections Data | Collection data files | COLLECTION_DATA | DISABLED |
| Reflection Data | API interfaces reflection data | REFLECTION | DISABLED |
| Database DDL operations | Results of DDL queries, such as describing tables or indexes | DB_DDL | DISABLED |
| EAV types and attributes | Entity types declaration cache | EAV | DISABLED |
| Customer Notification | Customer Notification | CUSTOMER_NOTIFICATION | DISABLED |
| Page Cache | Full page caching | FPC | DISABLED |
| Integrations Configuration | Integration configuration file | INTEGRATION | DISABLED |
| Integrations API Configuration | Integrations API configuration file | INTEGRATION_API_CONFIG | DISABLED |
| Translations | Translation files | TRANSLATE | DISABLED |
| Web Services Configuration | REST and SOAP configurations, generated WSDL file | WEBSERVICE | DISABLED |

## WHAT'S NEXT?

In this chapter, you completed a series of 12 tasks that help you start to understand Magento.

In the next few chapters, we're going to take a deeper dive into different areas that we saw while completing these task.

In the next chapter, "Simple Products Explained", we're going to focus on products. Let's show you how to create more advanced products.

# SIMPLE PRODUCTS EXPLAINED

The most important thing in your store are the products.

In this chapter, you're going to create your first product and learn about the key features of Magento products.

We're also going to show you how to categorize and organize your products.

In this book, we're going to be building a store called "Orangeville". The one thing that links all the products in the store is that they're a bright, Magento-themed, shade of orange. Hopefully you won't be sick of orange by the end of this book!

## CREATING SIMPLE MAGENTO PRODUCTS EXPLAINED

In the previous chapter, you created the first product. You added some carrots.

Now, let's go and add more orange products. We'll also explore some more advanced product options.

As always, we're going to be adding orange items to our store.

- Go to "Catalog", and then "Products".
- Click the big orange "Add Product" button.

Here are the details we're going to fill in:

- Product Name: **Pumpkins**
- SKU: **FOOD102**
- Price: **5.00**
- Tax Class: **None**
- Quantity: **100**
- Weight: **15 lbs**

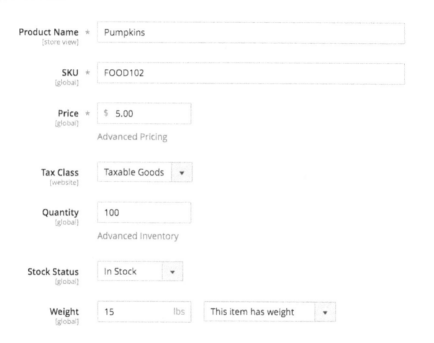

Now that we have more than one product in our store, let's create a special category for them.

- Click the "New Category" button:

- Category Name: **Fruit**
- Parent Category: **Default Category**
- Click the orange "Create Category" button.

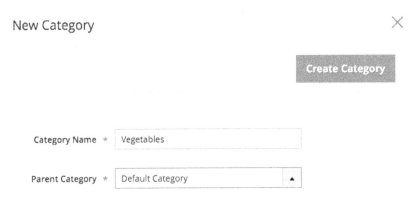

- You'll now see that this new category has been added for the Pumpkins:

- Open the "Images And Videos" slider.
- Click the "Browse to find or drag image here" button.
- Upload the pumpkins.jpg image from the "vegetables" folder in your downloaded Magento resources. That's available at http://ostraining.com/books/magento, if you need it.

960x640 px, 43 KB

Base   Small   Swatch

Thumbnail

- Click "Save & Close".
- You'll see a message that tells you that you saved the product.
  And, you can see both your Carrots and Pumpkins products.

Before we move on, let's make sure the Carrots are also in our new category:

- Click "Edit" next to "Carrots".
- Click the "Categories" field.
- Uncheck the "Default Category" option.

- Click "Save & Close".
- Visit the front of your site, and you'll see both products are now visible. Notice also that there is now a "Vegetables" link in the top menu. Categories are automatically added to this menu.

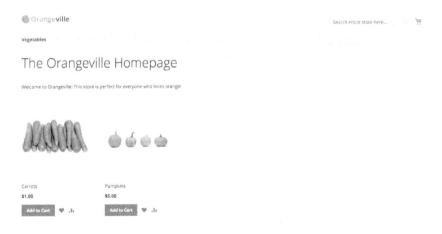

You might have already predicted that we would add this product, so let's go and add some Oranges as another product.

- Go back to "Catalog", and then "Products".
- Click "Add Product".

Here are the details we're going to fill in:

- Product Name: **Oranges**
- SKU: **FOOD103**
- Price: **2.00**
- Tax Class: **None**
- Quantity: **100**
- Weight: **1 lbs**
- Categories: Create a new category called "**Fruit**". Make sure the Parent Category is "Default Category".
- Set Product as New From: Choose a start date slightly before today's date and an end date slightly after today's date.

Now we're going to explore some more of the tabs underneath the main product options.

- Click "Content" and enter a description for the product. I entered, "**Orange is a citrus fruit that is delicious and high in Vitamin C.**"

- Click "Images and Videos" and upload the oranges.jpg image from the "fruit" folder you downloaded:

1024x768 px, 117 KB

Base  Small  Swatch

Thumbnail

Notice those 4 labels under the image? Here's what Base, Small, Swatch, and Thumbnail mean:

- Base: This is the main image you'll see on the product page.
- Thumbnail: This is the small image you'll see at the bottom of the product page.
- Small: This is used on pages with multiple products, such as your current homepage.
- Swatch: This version allows customers to rotate through images of multiple different product options. You'll see this again at the end of the chapter called "Configurable Products Explained".

Visit http://ostra.in/magento-images for more details on the image sizes.

So, one image can be shown in multiple ways across the site. You can also add videos to help promote your products:

- Click "Add Video" on the right-side of this area.

Images And Videos

1024x768 px, 117 KB

Base  Small  Swatch
Thumbnail

- Enter this into the Url field: https://vimeo.com/105467818

Url * | https://vimeo.com/105467818

Vimeo supported.
To add YouTube video, please enter YouTube
API Key first.

- Once you've entered that URL correctly, Magento will automatically pull in more details about the video.
- Click the "Save" button.

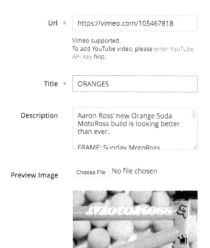

Url * https://vimeo.com/105467818

Vimeo supported.
To add YouTube video, please enter YouTube
API Key first.

Title * ORANGES

Description  Aaron Ross' new Orange Soda
MotoRoss build is looking better
than ever.

FRAME: Sunday MotoRoss

Preview Image  Choose File  No file chosen

Title:  ORANGES
Uploaded:  2014-09-07 04:18:29
Uploader:  Sunday Bikes
Duration:  00:00:43

- Click "Save & Close" to save your Oranges product.
- Visit the front of your site. You'll see your new product, plus the new "Fruit" category in the menu bar.

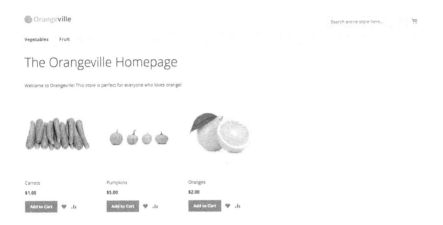

- Click on the "Oranges" box, and you'll see your new product page. Down below the main image, you can see the video you added. Click the video box and the video will play directly on this page.

## ADVANCED MAGENTO PRICING EXPLAINED

Let's add a fourth product to our store. This time we're going to experiment with some of the more advanced options in Magento products:

- Go to "Products", and then "Catalog".
- Click "Add Product".

Here are the details we're going to fill in:

- Product Name: **Mangoes**
- SKU: **FOOD104**
- Price: **2.00**
- Tax Class: **None**
- Quantity: **100**
- Weight: **0.5 lbs**
- Categories: **Fruit**
- Images and Videos: Upload the mangoes.jpg image from the resources folder.

## Images And Videos

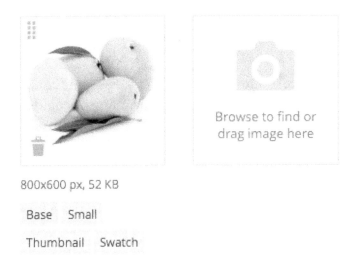

800x600 px, 52 KB

Base   Small

Thumbnail   Swatch

Now let's dive into those more advanced options.

- Click on "Advanced Pricing", which is under the main Price field:

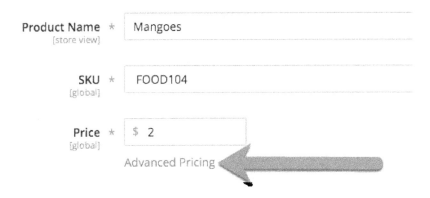

- A new area will slide in from the right of the screen:

The "Special Price" option allows to offer a discount for a certain length of time. Let's set up a discount that allows people to save 50 cents on mangoes:

- Special Price: **$1.50**

- Special Price From: Enter a start date and end date for your offer. In the image below, I'm offering a special price for the second half of 2018.

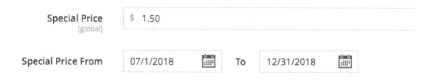

Now let's use another feature in the Advanced Pricing area. The "Customer Group Price" field allows you to offer different prices to different groups of customers.We're going to offer an even bigger discount on mangoes to logged-in customers:

- Customer Group: **General**

- Quantity: **100**

- Price **$1**

- Save your Mangoes product.

- Visit the front of your site and you'll see your Mangoes product.

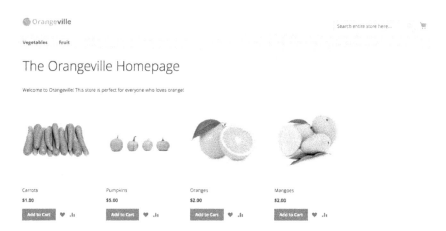

- Make sure you are logged out. If you are logged in, you can log out via the link in the top-right corner. Or you can just test your store in a different browser:

- Visit your mangoes, and you'll notice they're on sale for $1.50. That's the time-sensitive price that we established. In my example above, this $1.50 offer will only last until the end of 2018.

- Now log in to the front of your store using the customer details you created earlier. The mangoes now only cost $1. This is the "Customer Group Price" that we created.

So, let's recap what we did with Advanced Pricing:

- The normal price of mangoes is $2.

- The Special Price, for a limited time, is $1.50.

- If you are part of the "General" group of customers, you can get the mangoes for $1.

## RELATED PRODUCTS, UP-SELLS, AND CROSS-SELLS IN MAGENTO

Now that we have four products available in our store, we can use some more advanced pricing features.

Magento allows you to show additional products on a single product page. You do this in order to convince customers to buy more products, or just a more expensive alternative. Here are three options:

- Up-Sells: These are more expensive products you hope the customer buys *instead* of the current product. They show on product pages.
- Related Products: These are extra products you hope the customer buys in addition to the current product. They show on product pages.
- Cross-Sells: These are extra products you hope the customer buys in addition to the current product. They show on shopping cart pages.

Let's take a look at all three of these features in action. We're going to create a fifth product and add examples of all three selling options.

- Go to "Products", and then "Catalog".
- Click "Add Product".

Here are the details we're going to fill in:

- Product Name: **Peaches**
- SKU: **FOOD105**
- Price: **2.00**
- Tax Class: **None**
- Quantity: **100**

- Weight: **0.3 lbs**
- Categories: **Fruit**
- Images and Videos: Upload the peaches.jpg image from the resources folder.

First, let's create an up-sell. We're selling peaches for $2, but we would make more money if customers purchased pumpkins instead, because those cost $5.

- Click the "Related Products, Up-Sells, and Cross-Sells" tab.
- Click the "Add Up-Sell Products" button:

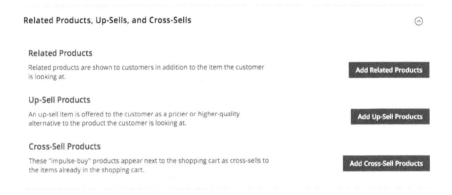

- Check the box next to Pumpkins and then click the "Add Selected Products" button:

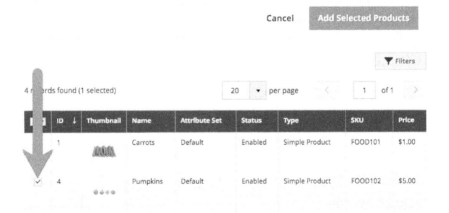

OK, great. We have an Up-Sell which is trying to convince the customer to buy a more expensive option. Now let's try adding a Related Product that the customer might be interested in in addition to the peaches. Our Related Product is going to be oranges, which are fairly similar to peaches.

- Click the "Related Products, Up-Sells, and Cross-Sells" tab.
- Click the "Add Related Products" button.
- Check the box next to Oranges, and then click the "Add Selected Products" button.

Finally, let's add a Cross-Sell. This is designed to be an impulse purchase during the checkout process, so the best option might be to choose mangoes, which are on sale.

- Click the "Related Products, Up-Sells, and Cross-Sells" tab.
- Click the "Add Related Products" button.
- Check the box next to Mangoes, and then click the "Add Selected Products" button.

When you've finished adding Up-Sells, Related Products, and Cross-Sells, you'll have all three listed on the screen, as in the image below:

**Related Products**

Related products are shown to customers in addition to the item the customer is looking at.

Add Related Products

< 1 of 1 >

| | ID | Thumbnail | Name | | Status | Attribute Set | | SKU | Price | Actions |
|---|----|-----------|------|---|--------|---------------|---|-----|-------|---------|
| | 5 | | Oranges | | Enabled | Default | | FOOD103 | $2.00 | Remove |

**Up-Sell Products**

An up-sell item is offered to the customer as a pricier or higher-quality alternative to the product the customer is looking at.

Add Up-Sell Products

< 1 of 1 >

| | ID | Thumbnail | Name | | Status | Attribute Set | | SKU | Price | Actions |
|---|----|-----------|------|---|--------|---------------|---|-----|-------|---------|
| | 4 | | Pumpkins | | Enabled | Default | | FOOD102 | $5.00 | Remove |

**Cross-Sell Products**

These "impulse-buy" products appear next to the shopping cart as cross-sells to the items already in the shopping cart.

Add Cross-Sell Products

< 1 of 1 >

| | ID | Thumbnail | Name | | Status | Attribute Set | | SKU | Price | Actions |
|---|----|-----------|------|---|--------|---------------|---|-----|-------|---------|
| | 6 | | Mangoes | | Enabled | Default | | FOOD104 | $2.00 | Remove |

Now that we have examples of all three promotional options, let's see how they look on the front of our site.

- Save the "Peaches" product and visit the front of your site.

- Click the "Peaches" product.

- Scroll down to the bottom of the screen. The "Related Products" is the first option you can see, together with a check box to easily add it to your cart. The Up-Sell has the text "We found other products you might like!"

## Related Products

Check items to add to the cart or select all

☐ Oranges

**$2.00**

♥ .ıı

## We found other products you might like!

Pumpkins

**$5.00**

- Add 1 peach to your shopping cart and click the "Add to Cart" button.
- Under the shopping cart icon, click "View and edit cart".

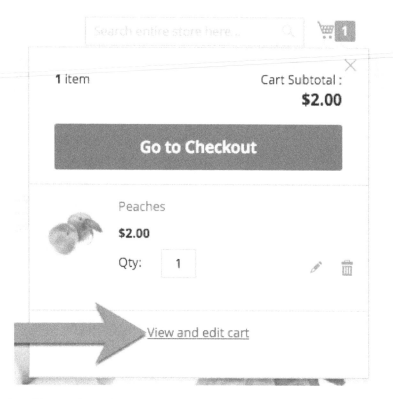

- You'll now be taken to your shopping cart, and your Cross-Sell is available under the cart.

# Shopping Cart

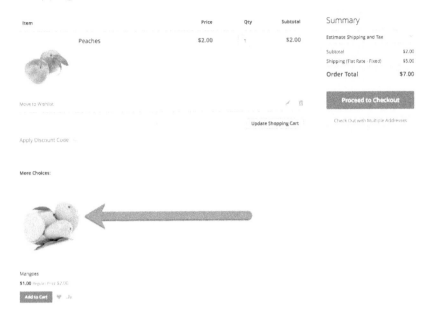

| Item | | Price | Qty | Subtotal | Summary |
|---|---|---|---|---|---|
| Peaches | | $2.00 | 1 | $2.00 | Estimate Shipping and Tax |

Subtotal — $2.00
Shipping (Flat Rate - Fixed) — $5.00
Order Total — $7.00

**Proceed to Checkout**

Check Out with Multiple Addresses

Move to Wishlist

Update Shopping Cart

Apply Discount Code

More Choices:

Mangoes
**$1.00** Regular Price $2.00
**Add to Cart**

## WHAT'S NEXT?

We've added 5 products to our Magento store. All of those products were "Simple Products". They were relatively straightforward products with standard fields, such as price, weight, and stock quantity.

However, we also saw how to configured some of the most sophisticated features for these products, included Advanced Pricing, Up-Sells and Cross-Sells.

In the next chapter, we'll show you how to customize your product details. Magento calls these details "attributes", and they include everything from price and weight to page layouts and gift certificates.

Add the end of this chapter, your Magento site will look like the image below. Don't worry if it's not an exact match. If you feel comfortable creating simple products in Magento, you're ready to move on to the next chapter.

Orange**ville**

Search entire store here...

Vegetables    Fruit

# The Orangeville Homepage

Welcome to Orangeville! This store is perfect for everyone who loves orange!

| Carrots | Pumpkins | Oranges | Mangoes | Peaches |
|---|---|---|---|---|
| **$1.00** | **$5.00** | **$2.00** | **$1.50** Regular Price $2.00 | **$2.00** |
| Add to Cart ♥ .Ii | Add to Cart ♥ .Ii | Add to Cart ♥ .Ii | Add to Cart ♥ .Ii | Add to Cart ♥ .Ii |

Privacy and Cookie Policy

Search Terms

Orders and Returns

Contact Us

Advanced Search

✉ Enter your email address    Subscribe

# PRODUCT ATTRIBUTES EXPLAINED

In the first chapters of this book, we added five products to our Magento stores.

These products had a price, a weight, an image and some other popular e-commerce options.

However, we used the same settings for each product. In this chapter, we'll see how customize our products. After all, everyone who reads this book has different needs:

- A book store will require fields for the Publisher, the Date of Publication, and the ISBN number.

- A clothing store may require fields for Type of Fabric, Clothing Size, and Clothing Color.

- A car store may require fields for Engine, Body Type, and Miles Per Gallon.

Magento allows you to add all those details through the use of "attributes". They are going to be our focus in this chapter.

## USING MAGENTO ATTRIBUTES EXPLAINED

Without realizing it, you have been looking at attributes throughout this book.

Any information you've entered for a product has been using attributes. Let's see what I mean:

- Go to "Stores", and then "Attribute Set".
- Click on "Default".

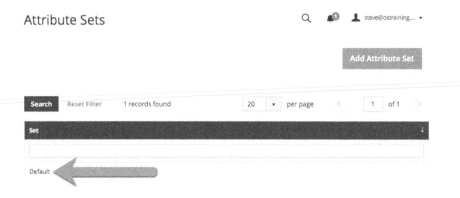

You now see a page with three columns:

- The left column is the name of this attribute set: "Default".
- The center column contains all the attributes that are being used.
- The right column contains all the attributes that are not being used.

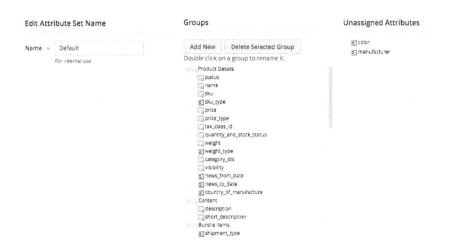

Let's see how we can add an extra attribute to our site.

- Drag the "manufacturer" attribute from the right column into the center column. Place it between "news_to_date" and "country of manufacturer".

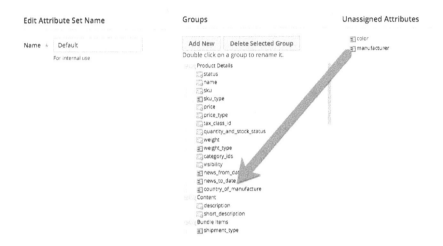

Now that we have two attributes that deal with manufacturing, let's group them together.

- Click the "Add New" button in the center column.

## Groups

- Enter "Manfacturing".
- Click the "OK" button.

- Your new "Manfacturing" group will appear at the bottom of the center column:

- Drag-and-drop the "Manfacturing" group up the center column, so it is positioned just above the "Content" group:

- Move both "manufacturer" and "country_of_manufacturer" into your new "Manufacturing" group:

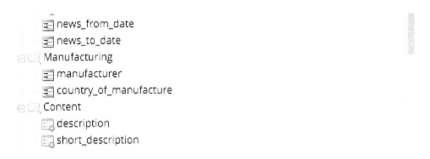

Great! You now have a new attribute group. Let's go and see how it appears when we're editing products.

- Go to "Products", and then "Catalog".

- Click "Edit" next to "Oranges".

- Scroll down, and you'll see a new "Manfacturing" area:

You will notice that the "Manufacturer" fields is empty and can't be chosen. However, you can choose "Spain" from the "Country of Manufacture" dropdown:

The Manufacturer field is provided by default with Magento, but it doesn't yet contain any choices. Let's solve that next.

- Click "Save & Close" for the Oranges product on your current screen.
- Go to "Stores", and then "Product".
- Scroll down on this screen, and click on the "Manufacturer" row.
- Enter options for the Manufacturer field. I've chosen three fake companies:
  - **Big Orange Corp**
  - **Big Mango Corp**
  - **Big Peaches Corp**

Manage Options (Values of Your Attribute)

| | Is Default | Admin* | Default Store View | |
|---|---|---|---|---|
| | ○ | Big Orange Corp | | Delete |
| | ○ | Big Mango Corp | | Delete |
| | ○ | Big Peaches Corp | | Delete |

Add Option

- Save the attribute.
- Go to "Catalog", and then "Products".
- Edit the "Oranges" product.
- Update the "Manufacturer" field:

Manufacturing

| Manufacturer [global] | Big Orange Corp ▼ |
|---|---|
| Country of Manufacture [website] | Spain ▼ |

- Click "Save & Close".
- Go to visit the front of your site and check the "Oranges" product page.

Can you see the Manufacturing details you just added?

No, not yet.

We have more work to do before our attributes are visible.

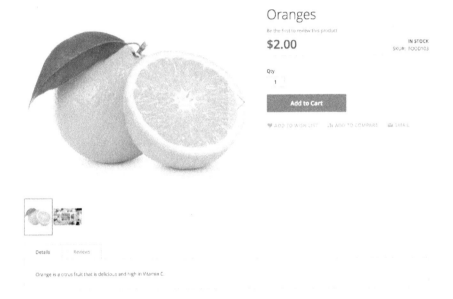

## DISPLAYING MAGENTO ATTRIBUTES EXPLAINED

Now that we've created attributes, let's make them visible on the site:

- Go to "Stores", and then "Product".
- Take a look at the table of attributes. Notice that the "Country of Manufacture" has "No" in the "Visible" column:

| Attribute Code | ↓ | Default Label | Required | System | Visible |
|---|---|---|---|---|---|
| | | | ▼ | ▼ | ▼ |
| category_ids | | Categories | No | Yes | No |
| clothing_color | | Clothing Color | No | No | No |
| color | | Color | No | No | No |
| cost | | Cost | No | No | No |
| country_of_manufacture | | Country of Manufacture | No | Yes | No |

- Click on the "Country of Manufacture" row.

- Click the "Storefront Properties" tab.

- Set "Visible on Catalog Pages on Storefront" to "Yes".

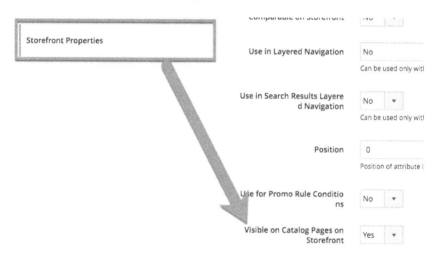

- Repeat that process for the "Manufacturer" attribute.

- When you look at your attributes table again, both "Country of Manufacture" and "Manufacturer" will have "Yes" in the "Visible" column:

| Attribute Code | Default Label | Required | System | Visible |
|---|---|---|---|---|
| | | ▼ | ▼ | ▼ |
| category_ids | Categories | No | Yes | No |
| clothing_color | Clothing Color | No | | No |
| color | Color | No | No | No |
| cost | Cost | No | No | No |
| country_of_manufacture | Country of Manufacture | No | Yes | Yes |

- Go to the front of your site and visit the "Oranges" product. You'll see a new tab called "More Information". This area contains your attributes:

| | |
|---|---|
| **Manufacturer** | Big Orange Corp |
| **Country of Manufacture** | Spain |

## CREATING NEW MAGENTO ATTRIBUTES EXPLAINED

In our first example, we used two existing attributes: "Country of Manufacture" and "Manufacturer".

In this next example, let's create a new attribute for our products. This is going to be "Farming Method", and the two choices will be "Organic" and "Non-Organic".

- Go to "Stores", and then "Product".
- Click "Add New Attribute".
- Default Label: **Farming Method**

- Catalog Input Type for Store Owner: **Dropdown**

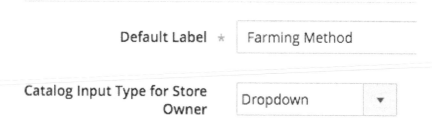

## Attribute Properties

Default Label   &#42;   Farming Method

Catalog Input Type for Store Owner     Dropdown ▼

- Add "Organic" and "Non-Organic" as options:

Manage Options (Values of Your Attribute)

| Is Default | Admin* | Default Store View | |
|---|---|---|---|
| | Organic | | Delete |
| | Non-Organic | | Delete |

Add Option

- Click the "Storefront Properties" tab.
- Set "Visible on Catalog Pages on Storefront" to "Yes".
- Save the attribute.

Our next step is to place the new attribute into the correct place in the editing screen:

- Go to "Stores", and then "Attribute Sets".
- Edit the "Default" attribute set.
- Move the "farming_method" attribute from the right column into the "Manufacturing" group.

**Groups**                                    **Unassigned Attributes**

| Add New | Delete Selected Group |

Double click on a group to rename it.

- Product Details
    - status
    - name
    - sku
    - sku_type
    - price
    - price_type
    - tax_class_id
    - quantity_and_stock_status
    - size
    - weight
    - weight_type
    - category_ids
    - visibility
    - news_from_date
    - news_to_date
- Manufacturing
    - manufacturer
    - country_of_manufacture
- Content
    - description

clothing_color
farming_method

- Click the "Save" button.

Let's go and see our new attribute in action inside a Product.

- Go to "Products", and then "Catalog".
- Edit the "Oranges" product.
- Make your selection from the "Farming Method" field:

**Manufacturing**

| | |
|---|---|
| Farming Method [global] | Organic |
| Manufacturer [global] | Big Orange Corp |
| Country of Manufacture [website] | Spain |

- Save the product and visit the front of your site. There is your new attribute:

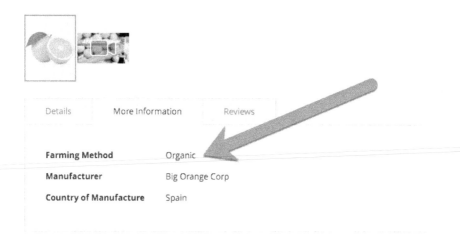

## SEARCHING WITH ATTRIBUTES EXPLAINED

Attributes are not limited to simply displaying data. You can also allow customers to use attributes to search and browse your store.

Go to the front of your site and click on the "Fruit" link in the main menu. You'll notice that there are filters on the left-hand side, including Manufacturer and Price.

How can you tell which attributes are available as filters?

- Go to "Stores", and then "Product".
- Look in the "Use in Layered Navigation" column. Any attribute with the text "Filterable (with results)" is going to be a filter.

| manufacturer | Manufacturer | No | No | No | Global | Yes | Filterable (with results) | Yes |
|---|---|---|---|---|---|---|---|---|
| media_gallery | Media Gallery | No | Yes | No | Global | No | No | No |
| meta_description | Meta Description | No | Yes | No | Store View | No | No | No |
| meta_keyword | Meta Keywords | No | Yes | No | Store View | No | No | No |
| meta_title | Meta Title | No | Yes | No | Store View | No | No | No |
| msrp | Manufacturer's Suggested Retail Price | No | Yes | No | Global | No | No | No |
| msrp_display_actual_price_type | Display Actual Price | No | Yes | No | Web Site | No | No | No |
| name | Product Name | Yes | Yes | No | Store View | Yes | No | No |
| news_from_date | Set Product as New from Date | No | Yes | No | Web Site | No | No | No |
| news_to_date | Set Product as New to Date | No | Yes | No | Web Site | No | No | No |
| options_container | Display Product Options In | No | Yes | No | Store View | No | No | No |
| page_layout | Layout | No | Yes | No | Store View | No | No | No |
| price | Price | Yes | Yes | No | Global | Yes | Filterable (with results) | No |

Let's make a change so that our new attribute is available as a filter:

- Click the "Farming Methods" row.
- Click the "Storefront Properties" tab.
- Change "Use in Layered Navigation" to "Filterable (with results)".
- Change "Use in Search Results Layered Navigation" to "Yes".
- Save this attribute.

- Visit the front of your site, and under the "Fruit" link your "Farming Method" filter is now an option:

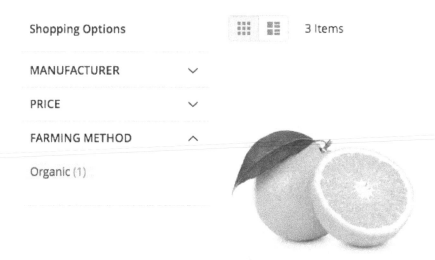

Shopping Options ⦙⦙⦙ ▦ 3 Items

MANUFACTURER ⌄

PRICE ⌄

FARMING METHOD ⌃

Organic (1)

### CREATING A NEW ATTRIBUTE SET EXPLAINED

There's one final topic to discuss about attributes. At the moment, all the products in the store have the same attributes.

We created an attribute called "Farming Method". But, what happens if we start adding orange clothes or furniture to the store? That attribute won't be useful at all.

Attribute sets allow you to show different attributes for different products. Let's see how attribute sets work.

In the next chapter, we're going to add clothes, rather than just fruit and vegetables. So, let's create give our "Default" attribute set a new name, and then create an attribute set for clothes.

- Go to "Stores", and then "Attribute Sets".
- Click on "Default".
- Change the "Name" to "Food".
- Click "Save".

## Edit Attribute Set Name

Name  *  Food

For internal use

- Click the "Add Attribute Set" button.
- Set the "Name" to "Clothes".
- Click "Save".

## Edit Attribute Set Name

- On the next screen, let's make sure we only use attributes that are relevant to Clothes products. Let's move the "farming_method" attribute from the middle column to the "Unassigned Attributes" column:

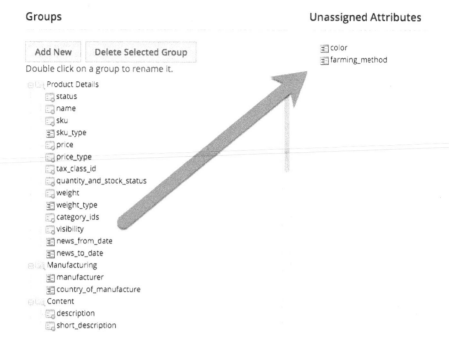

Groups

Unassigned Attributes

Add New    Delete Selected Group

Double click on a group to rename it.

Product Details
 status
 name
 sku
 sku_type
 price
 price_type
 tax_class_id
 quantity_and_stock_status
 weight
 weight_type
 category_ids
 visibility
 news_from_date
 news_to_date
Manufacturing
 manufacturer
 country_of_manufacture
Content
 description
 short_description

color
farming_method

- Click "Save", and then "Back". You now have 2 attribute sets. When you add clothes in the next chapter, you won't have to worry about the "Farming Method" field!

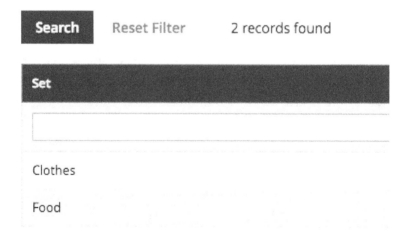

Search    Reset Filter    2 records found

Set

Clothes

Food

How does this work in practice? Whenever you're editing a

product, there will be an "Attribute Set" dropdown. You can choose the attribute set that's best for this product:

## WHAT'S NEXT?

We've added several products to our Magento store. All of those products were "Simple Products". To begin with, these were relatively straightforward products, although in this chapter we have added more details, thanks to attributes.

However, if you hover over the "Add Product" button, you'll see that Magento offers many more types of products. In the next chapters, we'll explore Configurable Products. These products use attributes to offer more complex product options.

**Add Product** ▲

Simple Product

Configurable Product

Grouped Product

Virtual Product

Bundle Product

Downloadable
Product

# CONFIGURABLE PRODUCTS EXPLAINED

We've created several products so far, and all of them have been "Simple Products".

Magento has six product types:

1. Simple Product
2. Configurable Product
3. Grouped Product
4. Virtual Product
5. Bundle Product
6. Downloadable Product

In this book, we're going take a look at all those product types. In this chapter, we start with Configurable Products.

Configurable Products rely heavily on attributes, so we're building on what we learned in the previous chapter.

## CONFIGURABLE PRODUCTS EXPLAINED

A Configurable Product has attributes that the customer can configure. Here are some examples of Configurable Products:

- A t-shirt that's available in blue, red, green and yellow.

- A jacket that's available in small, medium and large.

- A TV that's available in 20 inch, 30 inch and 40 inch sizes.

In Magento, these products would use attributes for different options. So this is how Configurable Products work in Magento:

- The t-shirt has a "color" attribute with blue, red, green and yellow choices.
- The jacket has a "size" attribute with small, medium and large choices.
- The TV has a "width" attribute with 20 inch, 30 inch and 40 inch sizes.

CREATING A CONFIGURABLE PRODUCT EXPLAINED

Let's walk you through the process of setting up Configurable Products. We're going to use peppers as an example. The peppers will have a "Food Skin Color" attribute with orange, red, green and yellow choices. Yes, it's sacrilege! We will have non-orange options for our customers.

There are three steps needed to create Configurable Products:

- Step #1. Create the Attributes
- Step #2. Create Configurations for the Products
- Step #3. Test the Configurations

**Step #1. Create the Attributes**

First, we're going to create the attributes that will form the basis of of our Configurable Products. Let's set up the "Food Skin Color" attribute:

- Go to "Stores", and then "Product".
- Click the "Add New Attribute" button.

Now we enter the details for our new attribute:

- Default Label: **Food Skin Color**

- Catalog Input Type for Store Owner: **Dropdown**
- Values Required: **No**

- In the "Manage Options" area, add the four options: Orange, Red, Green, Yellow.

- Open the "Advanced Options" area.
- Choose "Global" for "Scope". This setting allows your attribute to be used for Configurable Products.
- Click "Save Attribute".

**Advanced Attribute Properties**

Attribute Code     food_skin_color

This is used internally. Make sure you don't use spaces or more than 30 symbols.

Scope     Global ▼

Declare attribute value saving scope.

Now that we have the new attribute, let's add it to attribute set we're using for Food products.

- Go to "Stores", and then "Attributes Set".

- Click on "Food".

- Drag-and-drop your "food_skin_color" attribute from the right column into the middle column.

- Save the attribute set.

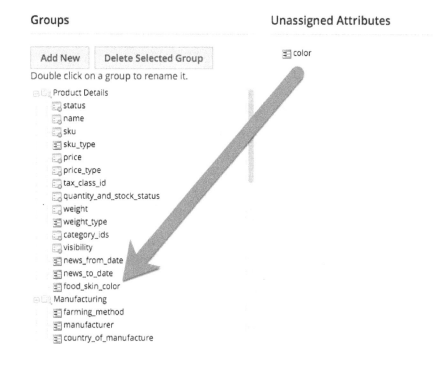

**Groups**

**Unassigned Attributes**

Add New    Delete Selected Group

🔲 color

Double click on a group to rename it.

- Product Details
  - status
  - name
  - sku
  - sku_type
  - price
  - price_type
  - tax_class_id
  - quantity_and_stock_status
  - weight
  - weight_type
  - category_ids
  - visibility
  - news_from_date
  - news_to_date
  - food_skin_color
- Manufacturing
  - farming_method
  - manufacturer
  - country_of_manufacture

## Step #2. Create Configurations for the Products

Step #1 was just did was simply a repetition of the last chapter. However, now we use our new attribute to try something new. Let's create our first Configurable Product.

- Go to "Catalog", and then "Products".
- Under the "Add Product" button, select "Configurable Product".

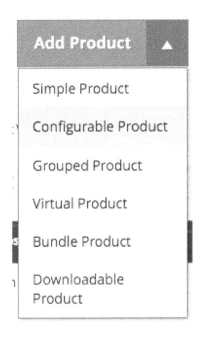

- Choose the "Food" attribute set.

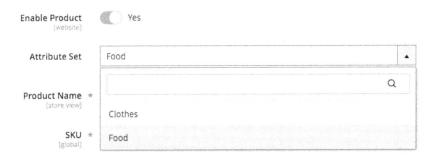

- Product Name: **Peppers**
- SKU: **FOOD106**
- Price: **3.00**
- Tax Class: **None**
- Quantity: **100**
- Weight: **0.5 lbs**
- Category: **Vegetables**
- Images and Videos: Upload the orange-peppers.jpg image from your resources folder.

450x350 px, 105 KB

Base   Small

Thumbnail

Now, we can use our new "Food Skin Color" attribute. Although we have multiple color options, this will be the default that people see:

OK, that was quite a lot of set up! We are now at the key point of the chapter. We can now create Configurations, which are the key to Configurable Products.

- In the "Configurations" area, click on the "Create Configurations" button:

- Your first choice will be to choose which attributes to use. Check the box next to "Food Skin Color" and click the orange "Next" button.

- On the subsequent screen, select all of your individual attributes, then click "Next":

- In Step 3, "Bulk Images, Price and Quantity", you can start to configure your new products, but I recommend you do that later. Click "Next" again.

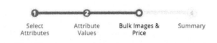

Step 3: Bulk Images, Price and Quantity

Based on your selections 4 new products will be created. Use this step to customize images and price for your new products.

- Now you'll see a table with an overview of the product you're about to create. Click the orange "Generate Products" button.

You are now back on the main product page. In the "Configurations" area you'll see the four new products. You can edit the details for each product.

- Upload the photos for the different pepper colors from your resources folder. You will find files called green-peppers.jpg, orange-peppers.job, red-peppers.jpg and yellow-peppers.jpg.
- Enter "100" for the "Quantity" of each product.
- Click "Save & Close".

| Image | Name | SKU | Price | Quantity | Weight | Status | Attributes | Actions |
|---|---|---|---|---|---|---|---|---|
| | FOOD10 | FOOD10 | $ 3.00 | 100 | 0.5 | Enabled | Food Skin Color: Orange | Select ▾ |
| | FOOD10 | FOOD10 | $ 3.00 | 100 | 0.5 | Enabled | Food Skin Color: Red | Select ▾ |
| | FOOD10 | FOOD10 | $ 3.00 | 100 | 0.5 | Enabled | Food Skin Color: Green | Select ▾ |
| | FOOD10 | FOOD10 | $ 3.00 | 100 | 0.5 | Enabled | Food Skin Color: Yellow | Select ▾ |

On your "Products" screen, notice what has happened. "Peppers" is a "Configurable Product", but Magento has also created four "Simple Products". Each pepper color is now a unique product. However, take a close look at the "Visibility" column: the Simple Products are marked as "Not Visible Individually". Only the main "Peppers" product will appear on your site.

| | ID ↓ | Thumbnail | Name | Type | Attribute Set | SKU | Price | Quantity | Visibility | Status | Websites | Action | Food Skin Color |
|---|---|---|---|---|---|---|---|---|---|---|---|---|---|
| ☐ | 8 | | Peppers | Configurable Product | Default | FOOD106 | $3.00 | 0.0000 | Catalog, Search | Enabled | Main Website | Edit | |
| ☐ | 21 | | FOOD106-Orange | Simple Product | Default | FOOD106-Orange | $3.00 | 100.0000 | Not Visible Individually | Enabled | Main Website | Edit | Orange |
| ☐ | 22 | | FOOD106-Red | Simple Product | Default | FOOD106-Red | $3.00 | 100.0000 | Not Visible Individually | Enabled | Main Website | Edit | Red |
| ☐ | 23 | | FOOD106-Green | Simple Product | Default | FOOD106-Green | $3.00 | 100.0000 | Not Visible Individually | Enabled | Main Website | Edit | Green |
| ☐ | 24 | | FOOD106-Yellow | Simple Product | Default | FOOD106-Yellow | $3.00 | 100.0000 | Not Visible Individually | Enabled | Main Website | Edit | Yellow |

## Step #3. Test the Configurations

Now let's see if our Configurable Products are working correctly.

- Go to the front of your site and visit the "Peppers" product, which will look like this next image:

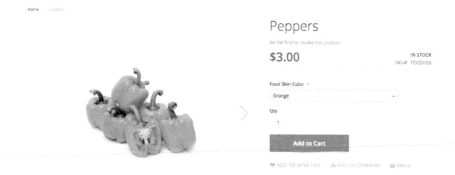

- On the right of the page, you'll see a dropdown field with your different attributes:

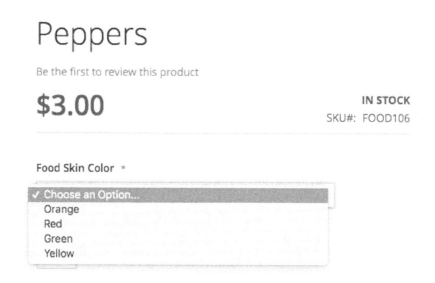

# Peppers

Be the first to review this product

## $3.00

**IN STOCK**
SKU#: FOOD106

**Food Skin Color** *

| ✓ Choose an Option... |
| Orange |
| Red |
| Green |
| Yellow |

- Change the dropdown choice and the image in the main area will change. Here's what will happen if you choose "Green":

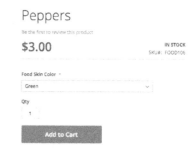

## CONFIGURABLE PRODUCTS TO CHANGE PRICES EXPLAINED

In our first example, choosing a different attribute didn't change the cost of the product. If you choose "Green", you get a different colored pepper, but pay the same price.

Let's see a different example of configurable products. This time our choices will have an impact on the price. We're going to create a Configurable Product called "T-Shirts". These will be available in different sizes, and each one will have a different cost.

**Step #1. Create the Attributes**

Let's create a "Clothing Size" attributes that we can use with our T-Shirts.

- Go to "Stores", and then "Product".
- Click the "Add New Attribute" button.

Now we enter the details for our "Size" attributes:

- Default Label: **Clothing Size**
- Catalog Input Type for Store Owner: **Dropdown**
- In the "Manage Options" area, click "Add Option" and enter these choices: **Small, Medium, Large**

- Open the "Advanced Attribute Properties" area.
- Scope: **Global**
- Click "Save Attribute".

Now, let's add the attribute to our "Clothes" attribute set:

- Go to "Stores", and then "Attributes Set".
- Click on "Clothes".
- Move the "clothing_size" attribute to the middle column.

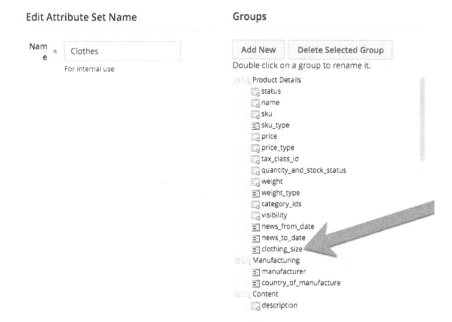

## Step #2. Create Configurations for the Products

Now we can go and use our new attribute.

- Go to "Catalog", and then "Products".
- Under the "Add Product" button, select "Configurable Product".
- Choose the "Clothes" attribute set.

Here are the details to fill in:

- Product Name: **T-Shirts**
- SKU: **CLOTHES101**
- Price: **10.00**
- Tax Class: **None**
- Quantity: **100**
- Weight: **0.5 lbs**
- Category: Create a new category called "Clothes". Make sure "Default Category" is the parent.
- Images and Videos: Upload the orange-tshirt.jpg image from the "clothes" folder of your resources.

The basic product details are in place, so let's use our attributes:

- In the "Configurations" area, click on the "Create Configurations" button.
- Click the box next to "Size", and then click "Next".
- Select all three attributes, and then click "Next":

- Click "Next" to move past Steps 3 and 4.

- Enter a different price for each size option. I used $10, $15 and $20.

- Enter "100" for each row in the "Quantity" column.

- Click "Save & Close".

| Image | Name | SKU | Price | Quantity | Weight | Status | Attributes | Actions |
|-------|------|-----|-------|----------|--------|--------|------------|---------|
| + | CLOTHES | CLOTHES | $ 10.00 | 100 | 0.5 | Enabled | Size: Small | Select ▾ |
| + | CLOTHES | CLOTHES | $ 15.00 | 100 | 0.5 | Enabled | Size: Medium | Select ▾ |
| + | CLOTHES | CLOTHES | $ 20.00 | 100 | 0.5 | Enabled | Size: Large | Select ▾ |

### Step #3. Test the Configurations

Let's test to see whether the prices really do change for our new Configurable Product.

- Go to the front of your site and visit the "T-Shirts" product, which will look like the next image. If you make a different choice from the dropdown, the price will change:

T-Shirts

Be the first to review this product

$15.00

IN STOCK
SKU#: CLOTHES101

Choose an Option...
Small
✓ Medium
Large

Qty

1

Add to Cart

♥ ADD TO WISH LIST    ⊪ ADD TO COMPARE    ✉ EMAIL

## CONFIGURABLE PRODUCTS WITH SWATCHES EXPLAINED

Let's see a third example of configurable products. This time, we'll show a small image under the product. Instead of using a dropdown field, customers can use these small images to make their choice.

We're going to use the example of a hat that's available in different colors.

### Step #1. Create the Attributes

First, let's set up a new "Clothing Color" attribute:

- Go to "Stores", and then "Product".
- Click the "Add New Attribute" button.

Now we enter the details for this new attribute:

- Default Label: **Clothing Color**
- Catalog Input Type for Store Owner: **Visual Swatch**
- Use Product Image for Swatch if Possible: **Yes**

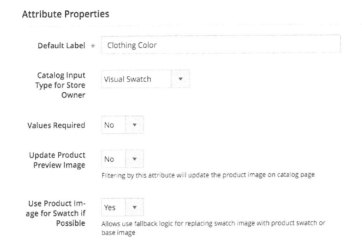

- Enter three swatch options: "Orange", "Pink" and "Yellow". Click "Add Swatch" to create each new row.

Manage Swatch (Values of Your Attribute)

| Is Default | Swatch | Admin * | Default Store View |
|---|---|---|---|
| | | Orange | |
| | | Pink | |
| | | Yellow | |

Add Swatch

- Open the "Advanced Attribute Properties" area.
- Scope: **Global**
- Save the attributes.
- Go to "Stores", and then "Attributes Set".
- Click on "Clothes".
- Move the "clothing_color" attribute to the middle column.
- Click "Save".

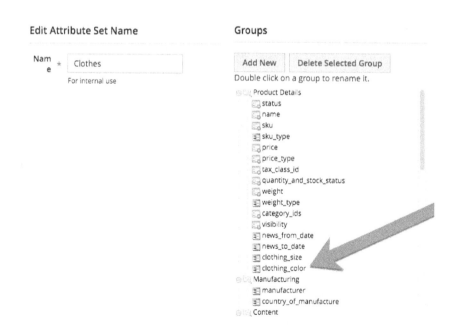

**Edit Attribute Set Name**

Nam ⋆ Clothes
e
For internal use

**Groups**

Add New | Delete Selected Group
Double click on a group to rename it.

Product Details
  status
  name
  sku
  sku_type
  price
  price_type
  tax_class_id
  quantity_and_stock_status
  weight
  weight_type
  category_ids
  visibility
  news_from_date
  news_to_date
  clothing_size
  clothing_color
Manufacturing
  manufacturer
  country_of_manufacture
Content

## Step #2. Create Configurations for the Products

Let's go and use our new attribute.

- Go to "Catalog", and then "Products".
- Under the "Add Product" button, select "Configurable Product".
- Choose "Clothes" for the "Attribute Set".

Here are the details to fill in:

- Product Name: **Hats**
- SKU: **CLOTHES102**
- Price: **15.00**
- Tax Class: **None**
- Quantity: **100**
- Weight: **1 lbs**
- Category: **Clothes**
- Images and Videos: Upload the orange-hat.jpg image from your resources folder.

1200x1200 px, 215 KB

Base   Small

Thumbnail

The basic product details are in place, so let's use our attributes:

- In the "Configurations" area, click on the "Create Configurations" button.
- Click the box next to "Clothing Color", and then click "Next".
- Select all three attributes, and then click "Next":

- Click "Next" to move past Steps 3 and 4.
- Upload the hat images from your resources folder.
- Enter "100" for each row in the "Quantity" column.
- Click "Save & Close".

### Step #3. Test the Configurations

- Go to the front of your site and visit the "Hats" product, which will look like the next image. You can choose different colors from the swatch images on the right, under the "Clothing Color" label:

It is also possible to display these swatches elsewhere on your site.

- Go to "Stores", and then "Products".
- Edit your "Clothing Color" attributes.
- Under "Storefront Properties", set "Visible on Catalog Pages on Storefront" to "Yes".
- Now go to the front of your site.
- Click "Clothes" in the main menu.
- You'll see that your swatches are visible on these category pages. The swatches can be displayed on other pages also, but that depends on your theme. We'll discuss themes more in the chapter "Magento Themes Explained".

2 Items

T-Shirts

**$10.00**

Pink

Add to Cart

## WHAT'S NEXT?

We spent an earlier chapter talking about Simple Products, and this chapter talking about Configurable Products. These are the most frequently used product types in Magento, so we covered them in detail.

However, Magento does have six product types in total:

1. Simple Product
2. Configurable Product
3. Grouped Product
4. Virtual Product

5. Bundle Product
6. Downloadable Product

In the next chapter, we're going to show you how to use those four remaining product types.

This image below shows what your site will look like if you've followed every step of the book so far. Don't worry if your site doesn't match this image perfectly. So long as you have a good understanding of Configurable Products, you're ready for the next chapter.

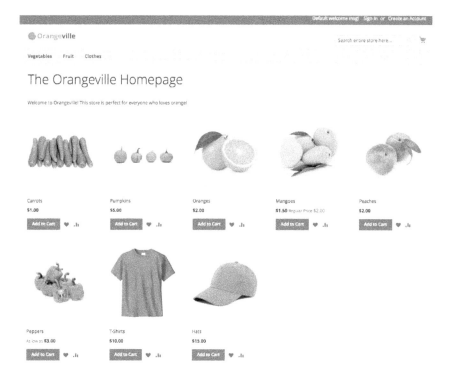

# GROUPED AND BUNDLE PRODUCTS EXPLAINED

Magento offers you the ability to create six different types of products:

1. Simple Product
2. Configurable Product
3. Grouped Product
4. Bundle Product
5. Virtual Product
6. Downloadable Product

So far in this book, we've discussed Simple Products and Configurable Products in depth. In this chapter, we're going to explain two more of those product types.

## GROUPED PRODUCTS AND BUNDLE PRODUCTS EXPLAINED

Grouped Products and Bundle Products are very similar, so we'll talk about them in the same section of this chapter.

- A Grouped Product is a collection of products. The customer can choose how much of each product they can buy.

- A Bundled Product is a collection of products.The customer can choose which products they buy.

Those are the technical explanations, but by themselves they are not very clear. Let's create both a Grouped Product and a Bundled Product so we can see the difference.

## GROUPED PRODUCTS EXPLAINED

Examples of Grouped Products could include:

- A "Basketball Uniform" product, with shirt, shorts and socks.
- A "Personal Computer Kit" product, with a keyboard, a mouse, a monitor, and a computer.
- A "Flower Planting" product, with seeds, a trowel, and a flower pot.

Let's create an example of a Grouped Product to show you how they work. We're going to create a "Fresh Fruit Basket" that combines all the fruits in our store.

- Go to "Catalog", and then "Products".
- Click "Grouped Product".

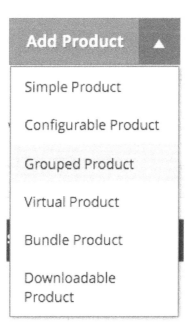

Enter these details for the new Grouped Product:

- Attribute Set: **Food**
- Product Name: **Fresh Fruit Basket**
- SKU: **FOOD107**

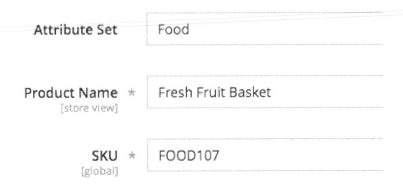

| Attribute Set | Food |
| --- | --- |
| Product Name * [store view] | Fresh Fruit Basket |
| SKU * [global] | FOOD107 |

Further down the page, let's add some more details for this product:

- Categories: **Fruit**
- Open the "Content" tab, and write this for "Description": **This product allows you to choose your own fruits for the gift basket.**

Now, let's choose the products that will be grouped together:

- Open the "Grouped Products" area and click "Add Products to Group":

**Grouped Products**                                                               ⌄

A grouped product is made up of multiple, standalone products that are presented as a group. You can offer variations of a single product, or group them by season or theme to create a coordinated set. Each product can be purchased separately, or as part of the group.                    **Add Products to Group**

- Check the boxes next to "Oranges", "Mangoes", and "Peaches".
- Click "Add Selected Product".

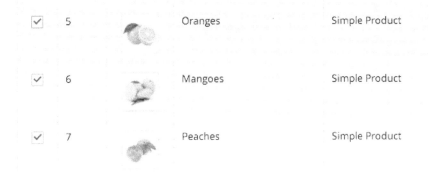

| | | Oranges | Simple Product |
|---|---|---|---|
| ✓ | 5 | | |
| ✓ | 6 | Mangoes | Simple Product |
| ✓ | 7 | Peaches | Simple Product |

- The selected products will appear in your editing screen:

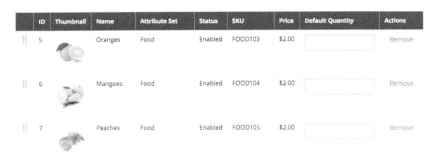

| | ID | Thumbnail | Name | Attribute Set | Status | SKU | Price | Default Quantity | Actions |
|---|---|---|---|---|---|---|---|---|---|
| | 5 | | Oranges | Food | Enabled | FOOD103 | $2.00 | | Remove |
| | 6 | | Mangoes | Food | Enabled | FOOD104 | $2.00 | | Remove |
| | 7 | | Peaches | Food | Enabled | FOOD105 | $2.00 | | Remove |

- I would also recommend opening the "Images and Videos" tab. Upload the fresh-fruit-basket.jpg image, plus an image for each product:

1796x1200 px, 428 KB     800x600 px, 52 KB     400x319 px, 10 KB     1024x768 px, 117 KB

Base   Small

Thumbnail

- Save the product, and then visit the front of your site. The Grouped Product will be visible. Notice that the price says "Starting at". That's because you can change the price by choosing the quantity of Oranges, Mangoes, and Peaches.

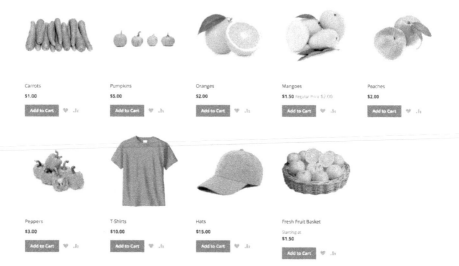

| Carrots | Pumpkins | Oranges | Mangoes | Peaches |
|---------|----------|---------|---------|---------|
| $1.00 | $5.00 | $2.00 | $1.50 Regular Price $2.00 | $2.00 |
| Add to Cart | Add to Cart | Add to Cart | Add to Cart | Add to Cart |

| Peppers | T-Shirts | Hats | Fresh Fruit Basket |
|---------|----------|------|--------------------|
| $3.00 | $10.00 | $15.00 | Starting at $1.50 |
| Add to Cart | Add to Cart | Add to Cart | Add to Cart |

- Visit the product page, and on the right-hand side, you'll be able to choose the quantity for each fruit. You won't see the final price you pay until clicking the "Add to Cart" button.

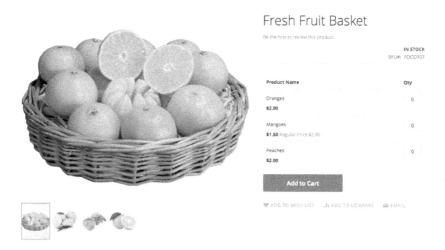

## BUNDLE PRODUCTS EXPLAINED

A Bundle Product is very similar to a Grouped Product. The only difference is that the customer can choose the products, rather than the quantity.

These are some good examples of a Bundle Product:

- A "Camera" product, where the customer can choose from multiple options, including "Camera", "Camera Case", and "Warranty".
- An "Airplane Ticket" product where the customer can choose from multiple options, including "Ticket", "Seat Upgrade", and "Travel Insurance".
- A "Book" product where the customer can choose from multiple options, including "Paperback copy", "E-book copy", and "Author Signature".

Let's walk you through the process of creating a Bundle Product. We're going to create a "Dress in Orange!" product that contains t-shirts and hats.

- Go to "Catalog", and then "Products".
- Click "Bundle Product".
- Attribute Set: **Clothes**
- Product Name: **Dress in Orange!**
- SKU: **CLOTHES103**
- Categories: **Clothes**

Look down the screen and you will notice that a lot of the settings for a Bundle Product are set dynamically.

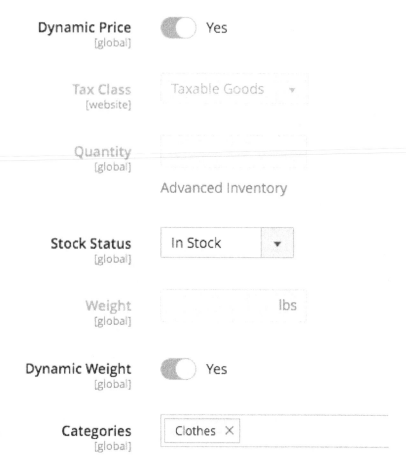

- Open the "Images and Videos" area and upload the orange-tshirt.jpg and orange-hat.jpg images.

1200x1200 px, 215 KB        1168x1200 px, 273 KB

Base    Small

Thumbnail

- Open the "Bundle Items" area and click the "Add Option" area.

Bundle Items

Ship Bundle Items          Together
[global]

Add Option

- Click the "Add Products to Option" button.

1    of 1

New Option

Option Title                Input Type
                            Drop-down          ✓ Required

Add Products to Option

- Choose the T-Shirts and the Hats.
- Click "Add Selected Products".
- You'll now see a screen like the one below, showing your two products.

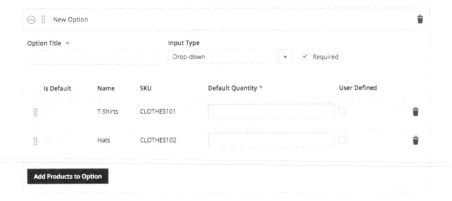

- Option Title: **Choose your orange clothes**

- Input Type: **Checkbox**

- Enter a "Default Quantity" of "1" for each product.

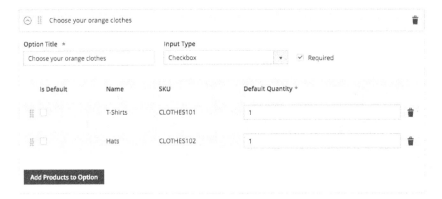

- Save the product and visit the front of your site. Notice that the Bundle Product is showing a range of prices, "From $10.00 to $25.00".

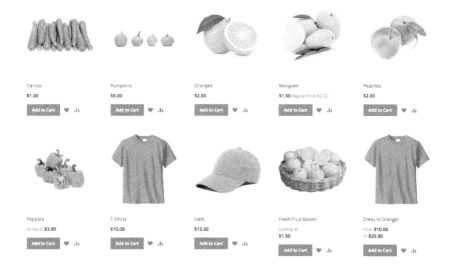

- When you visit the product, click the big "Customize and Add to Cart" button.

- As you check the boxes on the left of the screen, your price will automatically update on the right of the screen. Notice that, unlike Grouped Products, you can't choose the quantity for individual products. If you change the "Quantity" field, it will apply to all the products you've chosen.

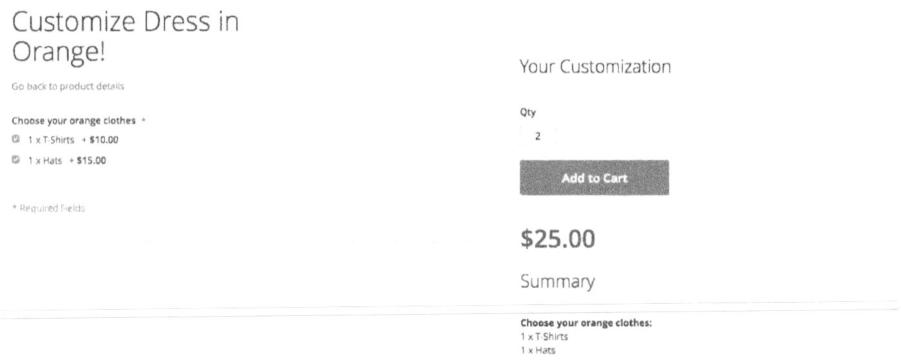

## Customize Dress in Orange!

Go back to product details

Choose your orange clothes *

☑ 1 x T-Shirts + $10.00

☑ 1 x Hats + $15.00

* Required Fields

## Your Customization

Qty

2

**Add to Cart**

## $25.00

Summary

**Choose your orange clothes:**
1 x T-Shirts
1 x Hats

## WHAT'S NEXT?

As we've mentioned a few times now, Magento offers you the ability to create six different types of products:

1. Simple Product
2. Configurable Product
3. Grouped Product
4. Bundle Product
5. Virtual Product
6. Downloadable Product

In the next chapter, we're going to explain the last two items on that list.

# VIRTUAL AND DOWNLOADABLE PRODUCTS EXPLAINED

In the previous chapter, we discussed Grouped Products and Bundle Products together because they are very similar. The same is true of Virtual Products and Downloadable Products, so we'll cover them together in this chapter.

- A Virtual product is a Simple Product, but without any shipping or weight information.
- A Downloadable product is a digital file.

Let's dig into specific examples of each so we can see how they are implemented in Magento.

## VIRTUAL PRODUCTS EXPLAINED

Examples of Virtual Products could include:

- Web design services
- Gym memberships
- Medical visits

None of those items require shipping, have a weight, or are tangible in any way. Let's see how to create a Virtual Product in Magento.

First, I'm going to recommend we create a new attribute set.

Neither "Food" nor "Clothing" options really meet our needs. Let's create a much simpler attribute set that doesn't have many of the attributes that you created specifically for Food and Clothes.

- Go to "Stores", and then "Attribute Set".

- Click "Add Attribute Set".

- Name: **Virtual and Downloadable**

- Based on: **Food**

- Click "Save".

Edit Attribute Set Name

- Drag all the attributes that you are NOT using over to the "Unassigned Attributes" area. For example, you can remove "clothing color", "clothing_size" and "farming method", plus others.

- Click "Save" and you'll see your new attribute set:

| Search | Reset Filter | 3 records found | | 20 | ▼ | per page | ⟨ | 1 | of 1 | ⟩ |
|---|---|---|---|---|---|---|---|---|---|---|

**Set**

Clothes

Food

Virtual and Downloadable

Now, let's create a new product that is entirely virtual. We're going to offer a service where we paint people's houses in a bright and beautiful orange color.

- Go to "Catalog", and then Products".

- Click "Virtual Product" underneath the "Add Product" dropdown.

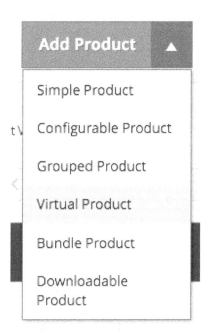

- Attribute Set: **Virtual and Downloadable**
- Product Name: **We Paint Your House Orange**

- SKU: **VIRTUAL101**
- Price: **$1000.00**

| Attribute Set | Virtual and Downloadable |
| --- | --- |
| Product Name *<br>[store view] | We Paint Your House Orange |
| SKU *<br>[global] | VIRTUAL101 |
| Price *<br>[global] | $ 1000.00 |

- Quantity: **1000**
- Categories: Create a category called "Services", using "Default Category" as the parent.
- Content: **We will paint your house in a bright and beautiful orange color. Your neighbors will love it!**
- Images and Videos: Upload the orange-house.jpg file from the "virtual-downloadable" folder.

780x487 px, 430 KB

Base    Small

Thumbnail    Swatch

That's really all there is to Virtual Products. These products are mainly distinguished by what they don't have. They don't have any shipping or weight options.

- Save the product and visit the front of your site.
- Click the "Services" tab in the main menu, click the new product, and you'll see this screen:

We Paint Your House Orange

Be the first to review this product

**$1,000.00**

IN STOCK
SKU#: VIRTUAL101

Qty
1

**Add to Cart**

♥ ADD TO WISH LIST    ⬩⬩ ADD TO COMPARE    ✉ EMAIL

## DOWNLOADABLE PRODUCTS EXPLAINED

Examples of Downloadable Products could include:

- PDF files

- Software

- Digital photos

None of those items require shipping, or have a weight, but they can be downloaded by the customer. Let's see how to create a Downloadable Product in Magento:

- Go to "Catalog", and then "Products".

- Click "Downloadable Product" underneath the "Add Product" dropdown.

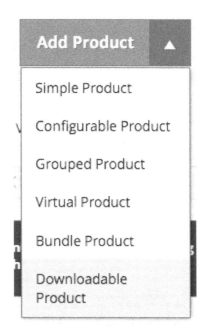

- Attribute Set: **Virtual and Downloadable**

- Product Name: **The Orange Book**

- SKU: **DOWNLOADABLE101**

- Price: $5

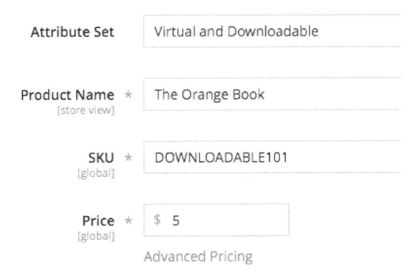

| | |
|---|---|
| **Attribute Set** | Virtual and Downloadable |
| **Product Name** *<br>[store view] | The Orange Book |
| **SKU** *<br>[global] | DOWNLOADABLE101 |
| **Price** *<br>[global] | $ 5 |

Advanced Pricing

- Quantity: **1000**
- Categories: Create a category called "Downloads", using "Default Category" as the parent.
- Content: "**This is the perfect book for anyone who loves the color orange.**"
- Images and Videos: Upload the theorangebook.jpg file.

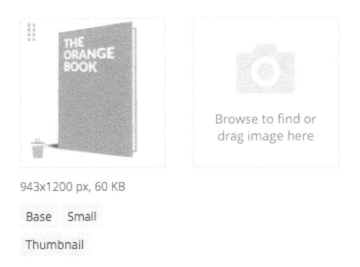

943x1200 px, 60 KB

Base    Small

Thumbnail

Now we can upload the product we're selling:

- Scroll to the "Downloadable Information" area.

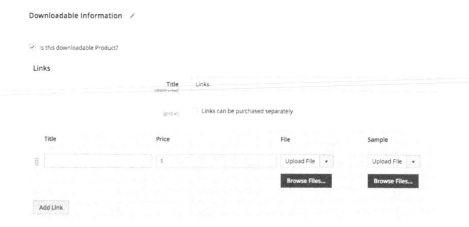

- Click the "Browse Files" button, in the "File" column:

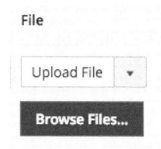

- Upload the file called theorangebook.pdf from your resources folder.

- Title: **The Orange Book**

- Save the product and visit the front of your site.

- Click the "Downloads" tab in the main menu, click the new product, and you'll see the screen below.

- When someone purchases this product, they'll be able to access the download from the "My Downloadable Products" section of their account:

## WHAT'S NEXT?

Up until this point in the book, we've focused mostly on products. After all, they are the most important feature in any store.

However, there is one important feature missing ... we can't take any payments yet. All our trips through the checkout have ended without us needing to open our wallet.

I suspect that the next chapter is why you got into Magento in the first place. Let's talk about payments, and how we take money for our products.

The image below shows what your site looks like if you've followed all the steps so far. Don't worry if you haven't followed exactly. You can still follow on with upcoming chapters. So long as you understand the topics we've covered so far, you're ready to move on.

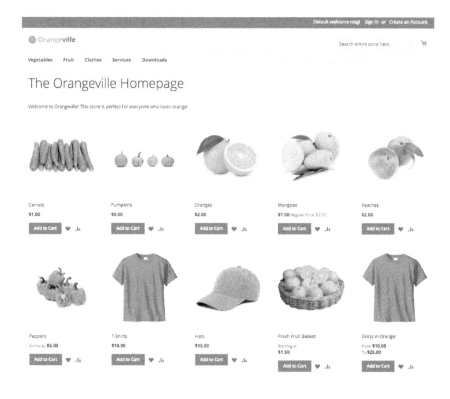

# MAGENTO PAYMENTS EXPLAINED

You have a store full of products, but you can't make any money yet.

It's time to add payment options to your Magento store.

Magento comes with several payment gateways, including PayPal, Authorize.net and Braintree. You have to activate them. Let's see how this works.

## MAGENTO'S DEFAULT PAYMENT OPTIONS

When you first set up your Magento store, two payment options are enabled:

- Check / Money Order
- Zero Subtotal Checkout

You've been through the checkout process, so you've seen how this works in practice:

- If the product has a cost, the "Check / Money Order" is used.
- If the product has no cost, the "Zero Subtotal Checkout" option is used.

In both situations, no money is taken from the customer.

## SETTING UP YOUR FIRST PAYMENT GATEWAY EXPLAINED

Magento's payment options are in the "Stores" menu link, alongside Taxes, Currency, and other financial settings.

- Go to "Stores", and then "Configuration".
- Open the "Sales" tab, and click "Payment Methods":

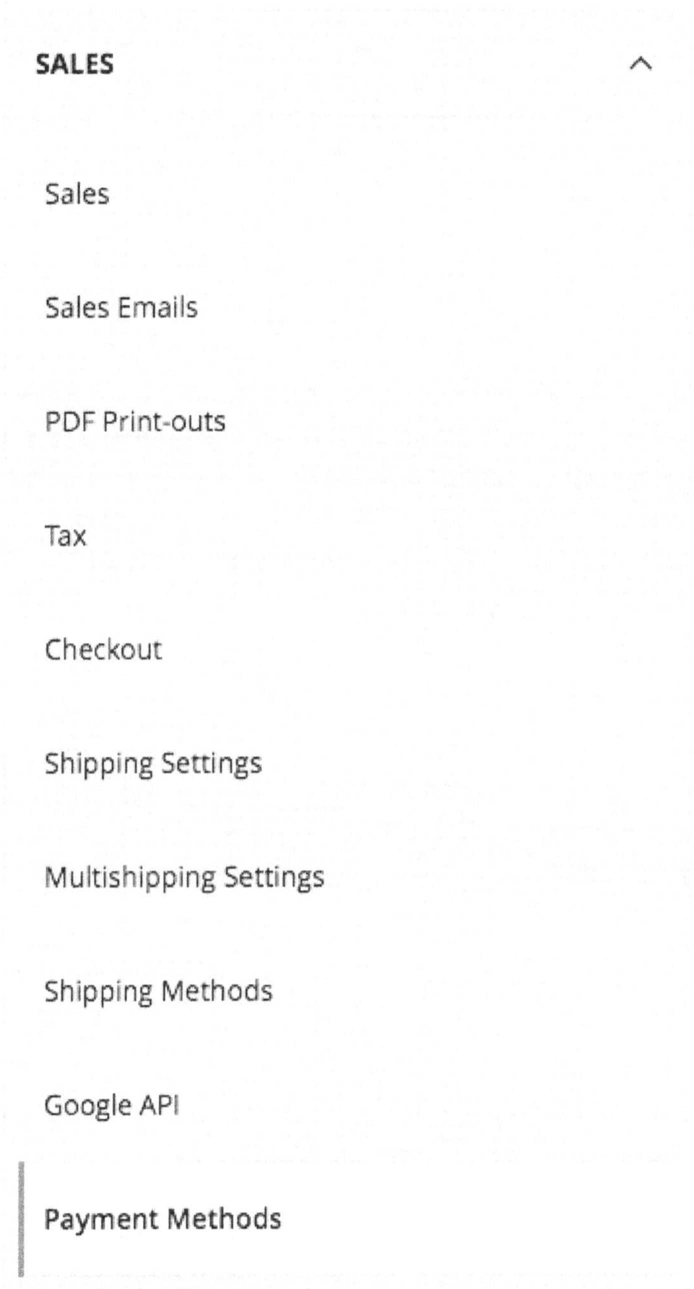

**SALES**                                    ∧

Sales

Sales Emails

PDF Print-outs

Tax

Checkout

Shipping Settings

Multishipping Settings

Shipping Methods

Google API

**Payment Methods**

You'll now see the default payment options available in Magento, divided into "Recommended Solutions" and "Other Payment Methods".

PayPal and Braintree are the two recommended solutions. Why did Magento provide these two as default options? In the first chapter, we mentioned that Magento was once owned by eBay. The same is true of PayPal and Braintree, so it made sense for eBay to recommend services from the same company.

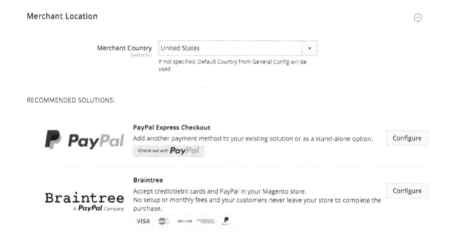

- Click on the "Other PayPal Payment Solutions" tab, and you'll see even more PayPal configuration options:

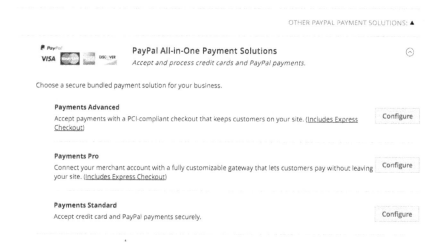

Further down the page, there are more payment options under the "Other Payment Methods" tab. With the exception of "Authorize.net Direct Post", none of these options connect to a payment gateway. Almost of these options require you to contact the customer and collect payment manually, outside of Magento.

As we mentioned earlier in the chapter, only two of these options are enabled when you first set up Magento: "Check / Money Order" and "Zero Subtotal Checkout":

If you include all the different PayPal choices, Magento arrives with thirteen payment options, of which two are enabled by default.

If you don't see the payment gateway you need, we'll show you how to add more gateways in the chapter "Magento Extensions Explained".

## ENABLING YOUR PAYPAL INTEGRATION EXPLAINED

Let's walk you though setting up PayPal to take payments in your Magento store. Before we begin, I have a few notes of caution:

- You will need a PayPal Business account to follow this part of the book.

- You will need the PayPal Express Checkout option enabled in your PayPal account.

- Magento has a reputation for having a difficult user interface. PayPal is far worse. My apologies in advance if your journey through setting up and configuring your PayPal account is much harder than we describe here.

OK, with those caveats mentioned, let's see if we can add PayPal to our store:

- Go to http://paypal.com and log in.

- Click "Configure" next to "PayPal Express Checkout".

You'll now see a form asking for your API details from PayPal. I'm going to show you two ways to get the credentials you need. The first option is easy, but doesn't always work, at least in my testing.

Here's the easier of the two options:

- Click "Get Credentials from PayPal".

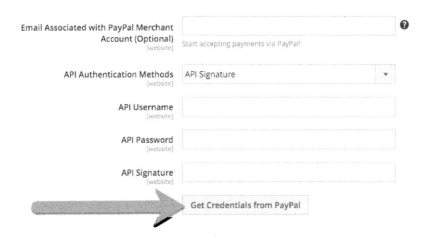

- PayPal will present you with a login screen. Log in to your account:

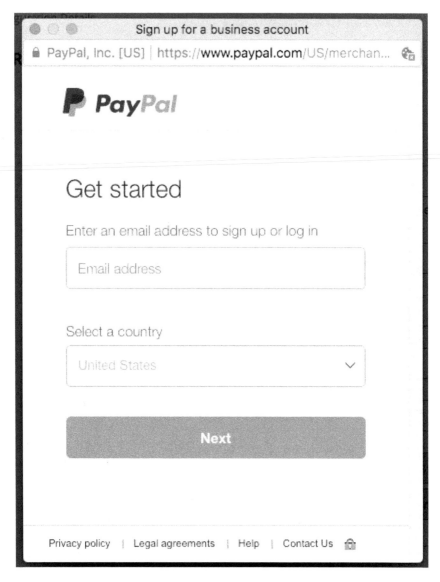

- After logging in, PayPal will attempt to automatically fill in your API details.

| API Username | •••••••••••••••••••••••••••• |
| :--- | :--- |
| [website] | |

| API Password | ••••••••••••••• |
| :--- | :--- |
| [website] | |

| API Signature | •••••••••••••••••••••••••••••••••••••••••••••••••• |
| :--- | :--- |
| [website] | |

If that first option doesn't work for you, it's possible to manually get your API details from PayPal. Here's the second option:

- Log in to PayPal.com.

- Click the "Profile" tab in the top-right corner, and then "Profile and settings":

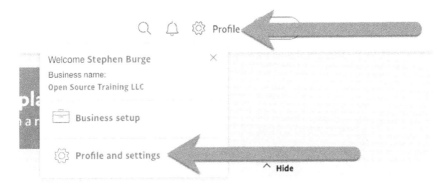

- Click "My selling tools" in the left sidebar, and then click "API access".

- Click "Manage API credentials" under the "NVP/SOAP API integration" tab:

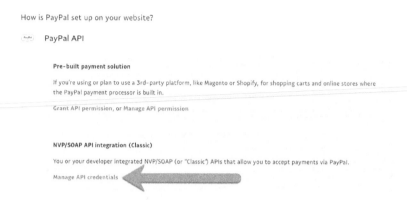

- You'll be taken to a page called "View or Remove API Signature".

- Click the "Show" links, and your API Username, API Password, and Signature will become visible.

- Now you can go back to your Magento site and manually enter your API details:

- Whether you chose the first or second approach, you can choose "Yes" in the dropdown "Enable this Solution".

- Click the "Save Config" button.
- Visit the front of your site, and there will be a PayPal button in the mini-cart in the top-right corner:

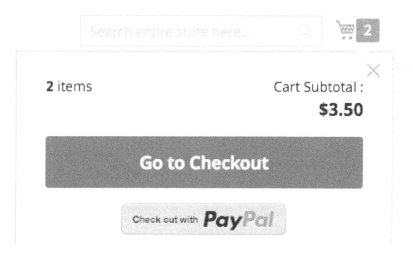

- During Step 2 of the checkout process, customers can choose how they want to pay:

 Orangeville

Shipping          Review & Payments

## Payment Method:

○ Check / Money order

 PayPal Credit  See terms

 PayPal Express Checkout  What is PayPal?

Congratulations! You can now receive money from your customer.

Each payment gateway has it's own unique steps that you must to through to enable integration. So, we've only covered PayPal in this chapter, because (for all it's flaws) it is still the most popular payment gateway.

If you're using another payment gateway, this is the best way to get started:

- Go to "Stores", and then "Configuration".
- Open the "Sales" tab, and click "Payment Methods".

- Click the "Configure" button next to your gateway and look for the information that Magento requests.

## DISABLING A PAYMENT GATEWAY EXPLAINED

By default "Check / Money Order" is an enabled gateway. If you do want to disable this or any other payment gateway, here's how to do it.

- Go to "Stores", and then "Configuration".
- Open the "Sales" tab, and click "Payment Methods".
- Open the "Other Payment Methods" area.
- Open the "Check / Money Order" area.
- Uncheck the "Use system value" box next to "Enabled".
- Set the "Enabled" field to "No".

## PLEASE GET AN SSL CERTIFICATE

Before we wrap up this chapter, it's important to mention that you will absolutely need one other thing before accepting payment.

You will need an SSL certificate. This protects the payment data as it travels between your site and the payment gateway. An SSL certificate doesn't prevent a hacker from attacking your site, but it does help protect your customers' data.

Once an SSL certificate is in place on your site, all your URLs will be available via https://example.com rather than http://example.com.

A good hosting company, such as http://Nexcess.net, will make it easy to add an SSL certificate. Contact your hosting company and see if they can help you add an SSL to your site.

## WHAT'S NEXT?

You've added products to your store, and now people can pay for them too. Wonderful!

If you need to add extra payment gateways, you'll need a Magento extension. Magento has a wide range of extensions that will integrate your site with different payment gateways. In the chapter called "Magento Extensions Explained", we'll show you how to find and install new extensions.

However, some stores do need to deal with two extra complications: Taxes and Shipping. In the next two chapters, we'll show you how to configure tax and shipping options for your customers.

# MAGENTO TAXES EXPLAINED

Welcome to one of the most complex chapters in the book.

We're going to try to explain everything in plain English, but there's no getting around the fact that taxes are a headache.

So, sit down in a comfortable chair and make yourself a strong cup of coffee. Let's explore how taxes work in Magento.

## E-COMMERCE AND SALES TAX EXPLAINED

There's really only one kind of tax that e-commerce stores charge: sales tax.

Sales tax rates are different in every country. For example, if we run our company from Florida, we need to collect 6% sales tax, at least on some products. In California, the sales tax is 8.25%. In the UK, sales tax is 17.5%. In Spain, it is 18% and in Denmark, the rate is 25%.

The name also changes from country to country. In many European countries, the sales tax is called VAT (Value Added Tax). In Canada and Australia, the sales tax is called GST (Goods and Services Tax). In Japan, sales tax is know as a consumption tax.

The name of the tax, the rate, and the surrounding rules will be different depending on where you are.

But, at the end of the day, we're all talking about the same thing. If you run an e-commerce store, you may well need to collect sales tax from your customers.

That's what this chapter is about. How do we calculate the right amount of sales tax to add to different transactions?

## THE BASICS OF MAGENTO TAXES EXPLAINED

If you buy a product from a Magento store, the sales tax you pay depends on "Tax Rules".

- Go to "Stores", and then "Tax Rules". You'll see this screen below:

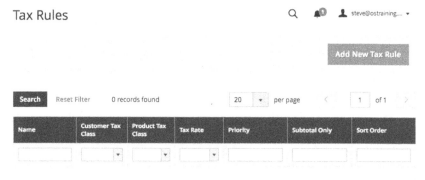

You will see that this screen is completely empty. We have no Tax Rules at all, so customers in our store will never pay any sales taxes. That's wonderful, right?

Unfortunately, that ideal setup would never last in the real world, at least if you want to stay out of prison.

So the focus of this chapter is on creating Tax Rules.

This is where it gets a little complicated, because Tax Rules consist of several different items. The image below shows the two different features that combine to create Tax Rules:

- Tax Classes: these determine whether you need to be taxed.

- Tax Rates: these determine the rate you may need to pay.

In this chapter, we're going to explain Tax Classes first, and then we'll tackle Tax Rates.

# Step #1. Tax Classes

Do products, customers and
shipping need to be taxed?

# Step #2. Tax Rates

Does the government charge tax
in the customer's location?

# Step #3. Tax Rules

This is what the customer is charged.
It combines the tax classes and
the tax rates.

## TAX CLASSES IN MAGENTO EXPLAINED

Tax Classes do not deal with money at all. Tax Classes simply answer whether you need to charge tax for the transaction.

Tax Classes can be assigned to shipping, products and customers:

1. **Shipping**: It's possible that your location requires that you add sales tax to shipping. This is true in over 30 states in the USA. Say you sold a $10 T-Shirt and charged $10 in shipping charges. In a state where shipping charges are taxable, the total taxable sale is $20, rather than only $10.
2. **Product**: It's possible that some products have a different sales tax rate. For example, in many locations, physical products require sales tax, but services do not.
3. **Customer**: It's possible that some groups of customers have a different sales tax rate. For example, in many locations, ordinary (retail) customers are taxed, but wholesale customers are not.

Here's how to find those three options inside Magento's configuration:

- Go to "Stores", and then "Configuration".
- Go to "Sales", and then "Tax" in the left-side menu:

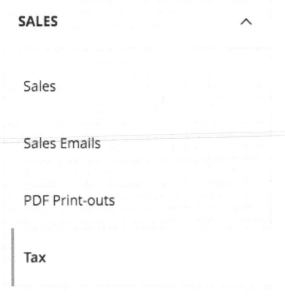

At the top of this screen, you'll see the settings for all three tax classes. So far in this book, we've been using these settings:

- **Shipping**: No tax.
- **Product**: "Taxable Goods" is the default, but we asked you to change this to "None" when creating products.
- **Customer**: Retail Customer.

So, what does this mean when a customer buys a product? It means that Magento has to perform several layers of calculations:

1. **Shipping**: If this product needs shipping, do we need to add tax?
2. **Products**: Does this particular product need tax?
3. **Customers**: You are in a particular group of customers. Do we need to charge tax for this group?

One of the things that makes taxes complicated is that you can't see them in action outside of the checkout. You can't see them until a particular customer has chosen a particular product to be shipped to a particular location.

TAX RATES IN MAGENTO EXPLAINED

This is where the government's accountants start to get excited. Tax Rates are Magento's way of collecting local sales taxes.

The Tax Classes are simply used to categorize the shipping, products and customers into "Taxable" or "Not Taxable".

The Tax Rate is where we explicitly define how much money should be collected.

Let's walk you through the process of setting up a tax rate.

- Go to "Stores", and then "Tax Zones and Rates".

- You'll notice that Magento already has two default Tax Rates available for California and New York:

| Tax Identifier | Country | State/Region | Zip/Post Code | Rate |
|---|---|---|---|---|
| | All Countries | | | From |
| | | | | To |
| US-CA-*-Rate 1 | United States | CA | * | 8.2500 |
| US-NY-*-Rate 1 | United States | NY | * | 8.3750 |

We're going to imagine our Orangeville business is located in Florida. After all, Florida is famous for oranges and orange juice. We want to collect a 6% sales tax from everyone in Florida who buys our products.

- Click "New Tax Rate".

- Tax Identifier: **Florida Sales Tax**

- Zip/Post Code: *

- State: **Florida**

- Country: **United States**

- Rate Percent: **6.0**

The Zip/Post Code option can be a little confusing. This allows you to set the tax for any Zip/Post Code that matches a certain pattern. For example, entering 9021* would cover all these zip codes: 90210, 90211, 90212, 90213, 90214, 90215, 90216, 90217, 90218, and 90219.

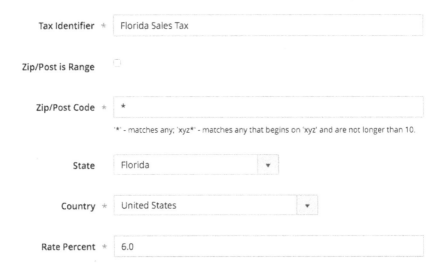

- Click "Save Rate" when you're finished.

- You'll see that your Florida Tax Rate is now visible alongside two more tax rates: 8.25% in California and 8.375% in New York.

| Tax Identifier | Country | State/Region ↓ | Zip/Post Code | Rate |
|---|---|---|---|---|
| | All Countries | | | From |
| | | | | To |
| US-CA-*-Rate 1 | United States | CA | * | 8.25 |
| Florida Sales Tax | United States | FL | * | 6.00 |
| US-NY-*-Rate 1 | United States | NY | * | 8.375 |

## CREATING YOUR FIRST TAX RULE EXPLAINED

So now we know the two key ingredients for setting up taxes in Magento: Tax Classes and Tax Rates.

Let's combine them into a Tax Rule that can actually be used during the checkout process on our store.

- Go to "Stores", and then "Tax Rules".
- Click "Add New Tax Rule".

We're going to set up a Tax Rule for the fruit, vegetable and clothing that will be shipped from our Florida headquarters.

- Name: **Products That Need Shipping from Florida for Retail Customers**
- Tax Rate: **Florida Sales Tax**

- Click the "Additional Settings" tab.

- Under these settings, you can see two of the Tax Classes: Customer and Product. We can leave these settings unchanged. If you did want to apply this Tax Rule to a different group of customers or products, you would change these settings.

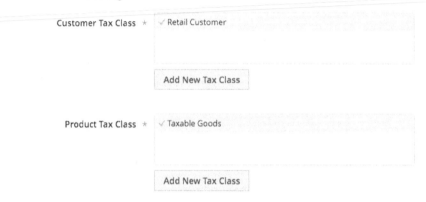

- Click "Save Rule".
- You'll now see an overview of all the Tax Rules. This screen only has the Tax Rule you created, so the only customers who will pay tax are those from Florida. We will need to create more Tax Rules for other states and countries.

| Name | Customer Tax Class | Product Tax Class | Tax Rate | Priority | Subtotal Only | Sort Order |
|------|--------------------|--------------------|----------|----------|---------------|------------|
| | | | | | | |
| Products That Need Shipping from Florida for Retail Customers | Retail Customer | Taxable Goods | Florida Sales Tax | 0 | 0 | 0 |

Let's see this Tax Rule in action. First, let's turn one of our products into a taxable product.

- Go to "Catalog", then "Products".
- Edit the "Carrots" product.
- Choose "Taxable Goods" as the "Tax Class".

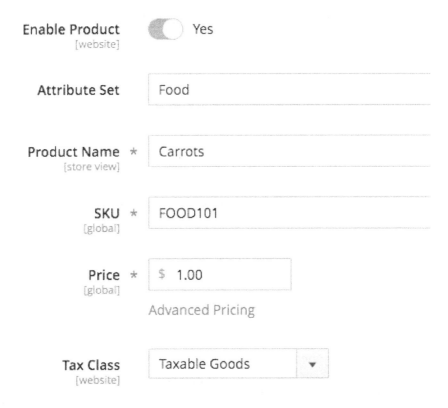

| Enable Product [website] | Yes |
| Attribute Set | Food |
| Product Name * [store view] | Carrots |
| SKU * [global] | FOOD101 |
| Price * [global] | $ 1.00 |
| | Advanced Pricing |
| Tax Class [website] | Taxable Goods ▾ |

Now let's buy some carrots and see if the tax is correctly added.

- Go to the front of your site.

- Sign in using your customer account.

- Go to "My Account" and edit your shipping address. It doesn't matter what details you add, so long as you choose "Florida" for the "State/Province".

- Click "Save Address".

# Edit Address

Contact Information

First Name *

OSTraining

Last Name *

Books

Company

Phone Number *

1234567890

Fax

Address

Street Address *

PO Box 110264

City *

Bradenton

State/Province *

Florida

Zip/Postal Code *

34202

Country *

United States

Now let's go and buy some carrots and pay some tax!

- Go to your store, and click "Add to Cart" for Carrots.
- Click through the checkout process until you get to the "Review & Payments" page. On the right-hand side of the screen, you'll see that $0.06 has been added for sales tax.

# Order Summary

| | |
|---|---|
| Cart Subtotal | $1.00 |
| Shipping<br>Flat Rate - Fixed | $5.00 |
| Tax | $0.06 |
| **Order Total** | **$6.06** |

1 Item in Cart ⌃

| | Carrots<br>Qty: 1 | $1.00 |
|---|---|---|

This first Tax Rule is a simple example, but hopefully it gives you a good introduction to how the system works. Tax Classes + Tax Rates = Tax Rules.

## CREATING MORE TAX RULES EXPLAINED

Let's take a look at some more examples of Tax Rules.

Florida is a state that does not charge Sales Tax for wholesale customers. So let's think through the example of a wholesale customer buying carrots:

- Shipping Tax Class: That remains on the site default of "None".

- Customer Tax Class: The customer is not charged any sales taxes.

- Product Tax Class: The carrots are a taxable product.
- Tax Rates: Florida charges 6% sales tax.

So what should our final Tax Rule be? The outcome is that the customer won't be charged any sales tax.

However, we need to specifically create a Tax Rule, or else they'll be charged the same 6% as retail customers.

- Go to "Stores", and then "Customer Groups".

You'll see that Magento provides four customer groups:

- General
- NOT LOGGED IN
- Retailer
- Wholesale

All of these have the Customer Tax Class of "Retail Customer". We can't create new Tax Classes here, but at least we know what Magento provides in terms of customer groups. We know that a "Wholesale" group already exists.

| ID | Group | | Tax Class |
|----|-------|---|-----------|
| | | | |
| 1 | General | | Retail Customer |
| 0 | NOT LOGGED IN | | Retail Customer |
| 3 | Retailer | | Retail Customer |
| 2 | Wholesale | | Retail Customer |

Our next step is to create the 0% tax rate.

- Go to "Stores", and then "Tax Zones and Rates".
- Click "Add New Tax Rate".
- Tax Identifier: **Wholesale Tax For Florida**
- Zip/Post Code: *

- State: **Florida**
- Country: **United States**
- Rate Percent: **0**
- Click "Save Rate" when you're done.

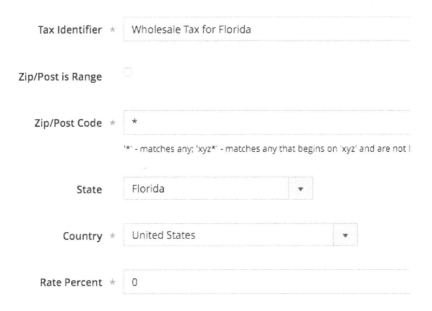

OK, so the first two parts are done:

- Tax Classes: We have a Wholesale Customer group.
- Tax Rates: We have 0% sales tax rate for Florida.

All we need to do now is create a Tax Rule and combine those two parts:

- Go to "Stores", and then "Tax Rules".
- Click "Add New Tax Rule".
- Name: **Products That Need Shipping from Florida for Retail Customers**
- Tax Rate: **Wholesale Tax for Florida**

- Under "Additional Settings", click the "Add New Tax Class" button.

- Enter "Wholesale Customer" and click the check mark.

- Select "Wholesale Customer" after it's been created.

- Click the "Save Rule" button.

Yes, this process was a little backwards, but we can now add the correct Customer Group to the correct Tax Class.

- Go to "Stores", and then "Customer Groups".

- Click "Wholesale", and then choose the "Wholesale Customer" group.
- Click "Save Customer Group".

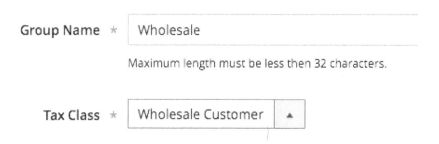

Congratulations. You've completed two examples of setting up Tax Rules in Magento. This is a big topic that would require its own book to cover in depth, but hopefully we've explained the key principles behind Magento's tax system.

Once your store is up-and-running, and you've received orders, you'll be able to find detailed reports on your tax obligations by going to "Reports", and then "Tax".

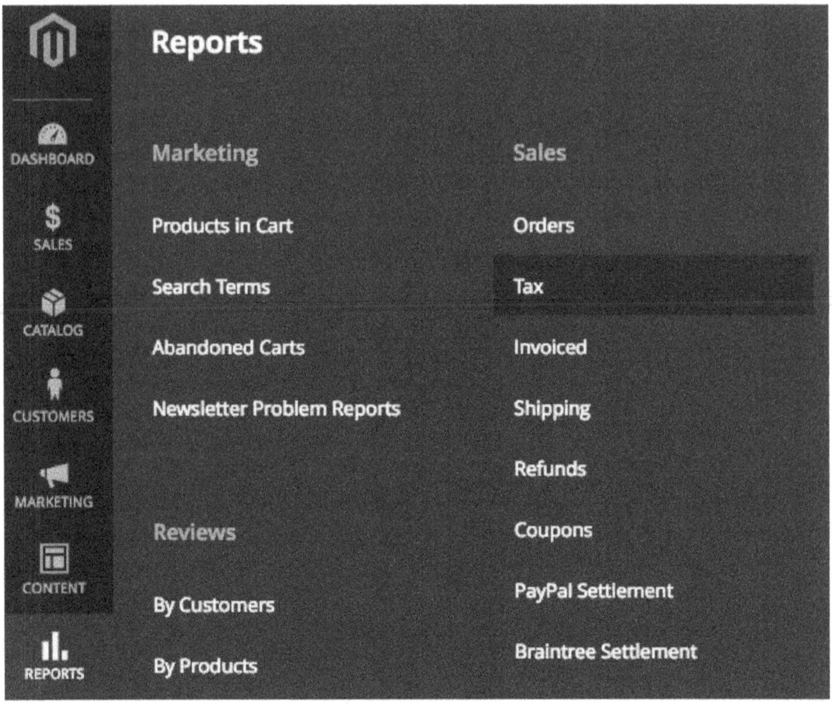
Reports
DASHBOARD
SALES
CATALOG
CUSTOMERS
MARKETING
CONTENT
REPORTS
Marketing
Products in Cart
Search Terms
Abandoned Carts
Newsletter Problem Reports
Reviews
By Customers
By Products
Sales
Orders
Tax
Invoiced
Shipping
Refunds
Coupons
PayPal Settlement
Braintree Settlement

## WHAT'S NEXT?

Remember the checkout process we saw earlier? The product cost $1.00 and the tax was $0.06. But the shipping cost $5.00! We need to fix that high price.

In the next chapter, we'll show you how Magento handles shipping for products in your store.

# Order Summary

| | |
|---|---|
| Cart Subtotal | $1.00 |
| Shipping<br>Flat Rate - Fixed | $5.00 |
| Tax | $0.06 |
| **Order Total** | **$6.06** |

1 Item in Cart ⌃

| | Carrots<br>Qty: 1 | $1.00 |
|---|---|---|

# MAGENTO SHIPPING EXPLAINED

So far in this book, we've created products that have a weight.

Customers can arrive at our store and buy those products, but at this point we have no way of delivering them to customers.

In this chapter, we're going to discuss shipping. If you are only going to use Magento to sell services and virtual goods, you can skip this chapter.

## ECOMMERCE SHIPPING EXPLAINED

Did I mention in the previous chapter that taxes were the most complicated part of this book?

Maybe I was wrong. Shipping might be more complicated still.

Shipping is not an exact science. It's closer to a series of guesses. Managing a successful shipping program involves many different variables. These variables include everything from the exact weight of the product and the shipping company's rates, to natural disasters and product returns.

Most eCommerce companies assume that they'll be slightly too high or low when calculating the shipping costs for each transaction. However, they're happy if overall they make a small profit, or cover their costs.

Some companies do try to simplify this problem (and attract

more customers) by offering free shipping. This is easier if you're Amazon.com. This is also easier if you're selling high-margin, low-weight products such as jewelry. Free shipping is harder to do if you're selling bulky, low-margin products such as t-shirts or heavy products such as furniture.

SETTING UP SHIPPING IN MAGENTO

Your first step to set up shipping should be to tell Magento where you're shipping products from.

- Go to "Stores", and then "Configuration".
- In the left-side menu, go to "Sales", and then "Shipping Settings".
- Uncheck the "Use system value" boxes and enter your address here.

Now let's choose the shipping methods that we'll offer to our customers.

- Still on the "Configuration" screen, click "Sales", and then "Shipping Methods".

There are eight shipping options in a default Magento store:

1. Flat Rate
2. Free Shipping

3. Table Rates
4. Magento Shipping
5. UPS
6. USPS
7. FedEx
8. DHL

| | |
|---|---|
| Flat Rate | ⌄ |
| Free Shipping | ⌄ |
| Table Rates | ⌄ |
| Magento Shipping | ⌄ |
| UPS | ⌄ |
| USPS | ⌄ |
| FedEx | ⌄ |
| DHL | ⌄ |

Let's walk you through some of these options and show you how they work.

FLAT RATE AND FREE SHIPPING EXPLAINED

First, let's look at "Flat Rate", which is the default option on our site.

- Click on "Flat Rate".

Here are some of the key settings:

- Type: **Per Item**. The shipping cost is charged for every item purchased.
- Price: **5.00**. This is the $5.00 shipping cost that we've seen in earlier chapters.

Further down the screen, you'll see the option to add a handling charge. This is currently empty:

You can also choose the countries where customers can choose this shipping option. Flat Rate shipping is currently offered to every country.

If you want to change any of these settings, uncheck the box "Use system value". For example, doing this next to the "Price" box will allow you change the $5 default:

| Price | 6.00 | | ☐ Use system value |
| --- | --- | --- | --- |
| [website] | | | |

The "Free Shipping" method is almost exactly identical to "Flat Rate". There is one exception: the "Price" field has been replaced by a "Minimum Order Amount". This allows you to provide free shipping only to customers who have spent a certain amount.

## TABLE RATES SHIPPING EXPLAINED

So far, everything has been relatively straightforward with Flat Rate and Free Shipping. Things are about to get substantially more complex with the "Table Rates" option.

This feature allows you to create a table of shipping rates in hundreds of different combinations.

The table below has a simple example of a table rate. In this example, we're defining the shipping cost for four countries.

| Country | Weight | Shipping Price |
| --- | --- | --- |
| U.K. | 0 | 3.99 |
| France | 0 | 6.99 |
| Spain | 0 | 7.99 |
| Italy | 0 | 9.99 |

Let's look at a slightly more advanced example. In this example below, we're defining the shipping cost for the United Kingdom. No longer does everyone in the U.K. get charged $3.99. Now they will have to pay more for heavier products. Any product between 10 and 14 lbs will cost $7.99 to ship.

| Country | Weight (and above) | Shipping Price |
| --- | --- | --- |

| U.K. | 0 | 3.99 |
| U.K. | 5 | 6.99 |
| U.K. | 10 | 7.99 |
| U.K. | 15 | 9.99 |

Weight is not the only criteria you can use to create table rates. This next table imagines a store in Italy. They want to increase the shipping price based on the number of items sold. Any customer buying between 10 and 14 products will need to pay $9.99.

| Country | Number of Items (and above) | Shipping Price |
| --- | --- | --- |
| Italy | 1 | 3.99 |
| Italy | 5 | 6.99 |
| Italy | 10 | 7.99 |
| Italy | 15 | 9.99 |

Often these Table Rates are created with software or a spreadsheet outside of Magento, and then imported.

Here's how to import these rates:

- Click the "Store View" dropdown in the top-left corner.
- Click "Main Website":

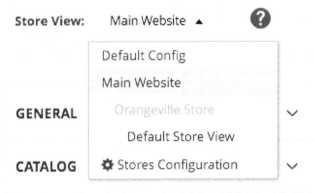

Inside the "Table Rates" area, there will now be "Export" and "Import" options. You can click "Export CSV" to get an idea of the format that Magento requires.

## MAGENTO SHIPPING EXPLAINED

Magento Shipping is a service provided by Adobe, via a company called Temando, to try and make shipping easier.

At the moment, Magento Shipping is not fully launched and you have to apply for access. Unfortunately, I can't recommend using Magento Shipping yet. At the time of writing, I have not heard back from them about two weeks after applying for access.

If you open up the "Magento Shipping" area inside your site, you'll see a link called "Request Shipping Account".

- If you click the "Request Shipping Account" link, you can apply for access to the service.

Create Account                                    2
                                    Shipping Information

## Create a Magento Account

Sign Out

**First Name** *

Steve

**Last Name** *

Burge

**Work Email** *

steve@ostraining.com

You can find out more about this service by visiting https://magento.com/products/shipping. They promise to provide shipping services that will benefit large, multinational organizations. Here are some of the promises on their sales page:

- Display convenient, competitively priced shipping options.
- More quickly and easily service international markets through out-of-the-box access and account registration.
- Configure shipping options and fulfillment automation rules directly from the Magento admin.

### UPS, USPS, FEDEX, DHL SHIPPING EXPLAINED

These four shipping options require you to connect to external websites. However, they can pull in live shipping rates, so they should be extremely accurate.

UPS is the only one that doesn't require us to create an account, so we'll use it as an example.

- In the "UPS" area, uncheck "Use Default".
- Enabled for Checkout: **Yes**.

- Click "Save Config".

Enabled for Checkout   Yes   ▾      ☐ Use Default
[website]

- Go to the front of your store and log in using your customer account.
- Add some Carrots to your cart and go through the checkout process.
- On the first page of the checkout, called "Shipping", you'll see that UPS has automatically created shipping choices for you:

## Shipping Methods

| | | | |
|---|---|---|---|
| ⦿ | $10.00 | Fixed | Flat Rate |
| ○ | $9.08 | Ground | United Parcel Service |
| ○ | $15.75 | 3 Day Select | United Parcel Service |
| ○ | $22.56 | 2nd Day Air | United Parcel Service |
| ○ | $31.59 | Next Day Air Saver | United Parcel Service |
| ○ | $34.71 | Next Day Air | United Parcel Service |
| ○ | $66.43 | Next Day Air Early AM | United Parcel Service |

## SHIPPING YOUR PRODUCTS EXPLAINED

Completing the transaction and collecting the money is only the first part of this process. Next, you need to ship the product.

- Go to "Catalog", and then "Orders".

- Click "View" next to the product that has just been paid for.

- Click "Ship" in the top-right corner of the screen:

- On this next screen you can enter the details of the shipment. For example, you can add the tracking number:

- Click the "Submit Shipment" button in the bottom-right corner.

- You'll now be asked to create the shipping package. First you define the height, width, length and other details for the package:

- Click the "Add Products to Package" button.

- Choose the products that were ordered.

- Click the "Add Selected Product(s) to Package" button.

- Click "Save".

Package 1      **Add Selected Product(s) to Package**

| Type | Total Weight | Length | Width | Height | | Signature Confirmation | |
|---|---|---|---|---|---|---|---|
| Customer Pa ▼ | 5   lb ▼ | 5 | 5 | 5 | in ▼ | Not Rec ▼ | 🗑 |

| ☑ | Product Name | Weight | Qty Ordered | Qty |
|---|---|---|---|---|
| ✓ | Carrots | 0.2000 | 2 | 2 |

Magento will now connect to the shipping carrier system, submit the order, and receive a shipping label and tracking number for each package.

You can print the shipping label and add it to your package.

Congratulations. You have created a product, received payment, and are now all ready to ship it to your customer!

Magento continues to help you, even after you have added the shipping label to your product and sent it to the customer.

- Go to "Sales", and then "Shipping". On this screen, you'll be able to track all your packages.

WHAT'S NEXT?

Up until this point of the book, we've explained all the key features you need to know to kickstart your Magento store. You know how Magento handles products, payments and shipping.

However, our store still looks ugly. It's not enough to have a working store. It also needs to look attractive and trustworthy for customers. In the next few chapters, we'll turn our attention towards building a great-looking Magento website. We'll add new features, add extra content and redesign our store.

# MAGENTO EXTENSIONS EXPLAINED

So far in this book you've seen many of Magento's core features.

However, there's a wide range of extra features that you can add. In this chapter, we'll show you how to find, install and enable Magento extensions.

## THE MAGENTO MARKETPLACE EXPLAINED

The Magento Marketplace is home to thousands of extensions that can expand your store's capabilities. It is the key place to evaluate all the extra features you might want on your site. The Magento team is constantly updating, improving, and optimizing the marketplace. Magento users are always testing and providing feedback on the extensions. I wouldn't recommend going anywhere else to look for extensions.

Let's head over there to start this chapter. The Marketplace is located at https://marketplace.magento.com.

On the Marketplace, you will see extensions categorized into "Customer Support", "Payments & Security", "Marketing" and other categories.

## Featured Categories

Customer Support    Payments & Security    Marketing    Accounting & Finance    Shipping & Fulfillment    Site Optimization

We do need to create an account on Magento Marketplace in order to install any extensions.

- Click "Sign In" in the top-right corner.
- Click "Register" and create an account on the site.

### Log In using your Magento Account

### Registered Users

If you have an account with us, log in using your email address.

\* Email

\* Password

Login

### New Users

It's simple and quick to register for a new account with Magento.

Register

- After you have created an account on the Magento Marketplace, come back to the screen above, enter your details, and click "Login".
- In the new dropdown menu, click "My Profile".

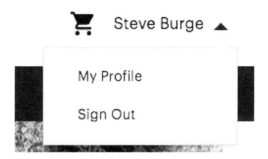

- In the "Marketplace" tab, click "Access Keys".

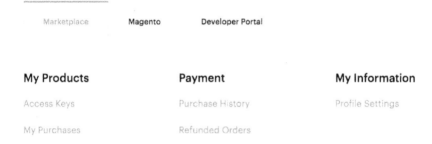

- Save a copy of your "Public Key" and "Private Key". We're going to need those to install our extensions.

- Now that you're registered with the Magento Marketplace, you can buy and install extensions.

## INSTALLING YOUR FIRST EXTENSION EXPLAINED

The Magento Marketplace has a lot of great tools for your site, but not every extension will work with your site. Be sure to use the search filters on the left side the page.

I recommend checking the boxes for "Magento 2" and "Community" to make sure we find extensions we can use. Remember that there are two versions of Magento, called "Community" and "Enterprise".

**Platform**

| | |
|---|---|
| ☑ Magento 2 | 65 |

**Edition**

| | |
|---|---|
| ☑ Community | 65 |
| ☐ Enterprise | 12 |

We're going to find an extension that will allow us to easily reindex our Magento site's data. An eCommerce site needs to store a lot of data, on customers, products, attributes, stock levels and more. In order to run quickly, Magento stores this data in a special format, known as an index. Without this, your site would run really slowly.

However, every time you make a significant change on your site, your data needs to be reindexed. Normally, this is a difficult task in Magento, but with the help of an extension, we can make the process much easier.

- Search the Marketplace for the extension called "Reindex From Backend".

- In the image below, click on the "Reindex From Backend" title. The URL for this extension is https://ostra.in/reindex.

Notice those stars underneath each extension? The extensions show feedback from people like you. Magento users are allowed to vote on extensions and leave their comments. The extensions that have the most positive feedback rise to the top. In addition to the ratings, Magento users can also leave reviews. At the bottom of the "Reindex From Backend" screen, you can see the reviews, including this positive feedback:

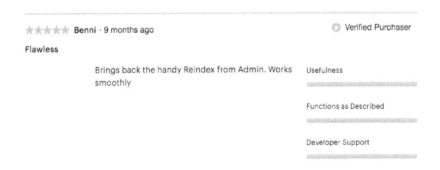

You may have noticed this particular extension is free. About 25% of the extensions on the Marketplace are completely free to use. The other 75% of the extensions are commercial, and you have to pay to download them. They generally cost from $30 up to $300 for the most advanced.

Regardless of whether you use a free or commercial extension, they all have two things in common:

- You can use them on as many sites as you want.

- The code is completely open. If you know how, you can change anything and everything about how they work.

Remember that developing extensions is hard and everyone has bills to pay. Almost everyone who writes code for Magento is able to do so because they make money from it in some way. Good developers can easily charge $100 to $150 per hour for their work, so the cost of these extensions is comparatively very affordable.

Free extension developers often make money by doing work for clients who need Magento help. Even free extension developers have business models: after all, everyone needs to pay the bills and keep their lights on.

- Some use the extension as a form of advertising to help them attract business. For example, someone might download a photo gallery, realize that they need an extra feature, and then hire the developer of the photo gallery to code that feature.

- Some do work for clients and then get their permission to release the code afterwards.

- Some rely on donations. If you use a noncommercial extension and see a donation button on the developer's site, it's good practice to send them some money.

- Some may sell premium versions of their free extensions with more features and high priority support.

Commercial extension developers make money by selling their extensions. They have a variety of business models:

- Some charge for the extension. Often paying for the extension gives you access to download it and any updates for a certain period of time, such as six months or a year.

- Some provide the main part of the extension for free and charge for extra features.

- Some give the extension away for free and charge for support.

Now that we've found our first extension, let's get a copy that we can use on our site.

- Click "Add to Cart".

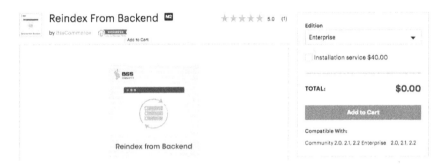

- You'll see a message that the extension was added to your cart, and you'll see the "1" icon in the top-right corner. Doesn't this shopping experience feel similar to your own Magento store? That's because the Marketplace is built using Magento!

- Complete the checkout process. Remember that this is a free extension, so you don't need to pay.

- Click "Place Order". You've successfully obtained a copy of this extension.

## Checkout

**Payment & Billing Info:**

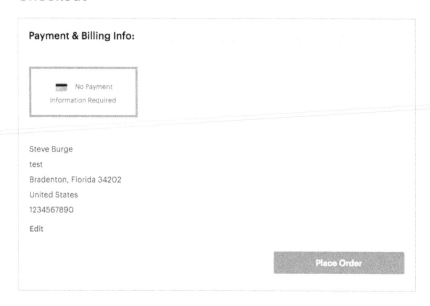

No Payment
Information Required

Steve Burge
test
Bradenton, Florida 34202
United States
1234567890

Edit

Place Order

Now that we have a copy of this "Reindex From Backend" extension, you can install it at your site.

- Go back to your site's Magento admin area.
- Go to "System", and then "Web Setup Wizard".

**Important**: Not every hosting company will allow Magento users to access the "Web Setup Wizard" area. Some hosting companies do disable access for security reasons. If you are not able to proceed at this point, please contact your hosting company. If you decide to use Nexcess, the hosting company we recommend, they do disable this feature also, but they have an easy and safe workaround.A good website builder never practices on their live site. You don't want to test out your changes on a site where customers can see your changes. So Nexcess provides you with an easy way to create a test version of your site where you can happily make all the changes you want. Plus if you break anything, you can always create a new test site. Follow the instructions here: https://ostra.in/dev-sites. Nexcess will create an exact copy of your Magento site with the same username and password. This development site is a great place to practice installing extensions.

- Click "Extension Manager".

- Enter the Public and Private API Keys you collected earlier from the Marketplace:

## Magento Marketplace

To upgrade or install purchases, enter your access keys

**Need to find your keys?**

1. Go to your Magento Marketplace account page.
2. On the "Access keys" page, copy your public and private keys.
3. Enter keys below:

* Public Access Key

```
c9c8e83581856e40e36a2e925
```

* Private Access Key

```
································
```

Sign in

- You'll now see an overview of your Magento extensions. Because you've only just installed your Magento site, there are likely to be zero updates available. However, if you do see any updates, we'll show you how to apply those updates in the chapter "Magento Site Management Explained".

- Click "Review and Install".

- Check the box next to "bsscomemrce/reindex-data".
- Click the "Install" button in the top-left corner.

Magento will now start to test your store to make sure it's ready for the installation.

- Click "Start Readiness Check". This may take a while, as Magento makes sure your server is ready to run this extension.

If your site is not ready, Magento will tell you what needs to change. For example, in the image below, you can see links to documentation that will help you resolve each problem. This troubleshooting can be tricky, because the documentation isn't always clear. To be honest, even after years of Magento experience, I sometimes struggle at this step, especially with new hosting companies. I recommend contacting your hosting company if you're having problems resolving these issues. An excellent Magento hosting company, such as http://Nexcess.net, should have your site prepared to avoid these issues.

**❌ Check Cron Scripts**
Cron script readiness check failed. Hide detail

For additional assistance, see cron scripts help.

**❌ Check Component Dependency**
We found conflicting component dependencies. Hide detail

For additional assistance, see component dependency help .

- Once your site has successfully passed the Readiness Check, click "Next".
- Magento will now offer to take a backup of your site. If you choose to take a backup, this may take a while because the default choice is to backup your code, media, and the database. You can uncheck these three boxes and not take a backup. We talk more about backups in the chapter "Magento Site Management Explained".

Readiness Check     Create Backup     Component Install

## Step 2: Create Backup

| Backup Options | ✔ Code |
|---|---|
| | ✔ Media |
| | ✔ Database |

Let's check your disk space availability for taking selected backups, and then create the backups.

Create Backup

- After the backup is done, you'll see the message: "Completed! You can now move on to the next step."
- Click "Next".

## Step 2: Create Backup

✓ **Completed!** You can now move on to the next step.

✓ **Disk space available**
You have enough space available in disk for taking your selected backups.

✓ **Store in maintenance mode**
Your store is in maintenance mode and will automatically return online after the install.

✓ **Backup created**
The backup files can be found in Magento Admin's backup management.

- You are now on the third and final step of the installation process. Click "Install". Please note that your site will be offline briefly as the installation completes.

## Step 3: Component Install

⚠ We will take your store offline to protect shoppers during the duration of the install activity.

- Once the process is complete, you'll see a "Success" message.
- Click "Back to Setup Tool".

Congratulations! You just installed your first Magento extension! Here's how to use your new "Reindex From Backend" extension.

- Go to "System", and then "Index Management".

- You'll now see a dropdown option called "Reindex Data". You can now select any of the indexes and easily reindex your data. If you want to learn more about indexing in Magento, we have a video and links at http://ostraining.com/books/magento/index.

## INSTALLING YOUR SECOND EXTENSION EXPLAINED

Let's try this extension installation process one more time.

The first extension helped to improve our experience as Magento administrators. This next extension will improve the experience for our visitors. We're going to make it easy for our visitors to ask questions about our products.

- Go to the Magento Marketplace. Look for the extension called "Product Question". You can find it at this URL: https://ostra.in/question.

- Go through the purchase process for this extension. As with the first extension, this extension doesn't cost anything.

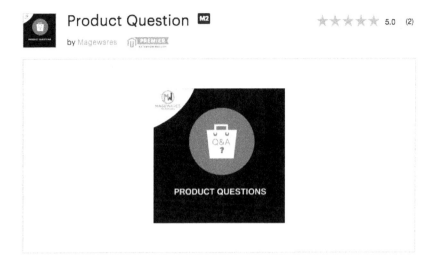

**Product Question** M2

by Magewares

★★★★★ 5.0 (2)

- Go back to the admin area of your Magento site.

- Go to "System", and then "Web Setup Wizard".

- Click "Extension Manager". You'll now see a list of the extensions you've installed, which will only be the "Reindex From Backend" extension.

- Click "Review and Install".

## Magento Marketplace Account Disconnect

| 0 Updates Available | 56 Extensions Ready to Install | Last Refresh at 12:33PM on 16 Jun 2018 |
|---|---|---|
| Review Updates | Review and Install | Refresh |

Installed Extensions 1 extensions

| Extension Name | Type | Version | Vendor | Actions |
|---|---|---|---|---|
| bsscommerce/reindex-data | Module | 1.0.1 | Bsscommerce | Select ▾ |

- Select "magewares/module-mwparent".

- Select "magewares/module-mwask-question".

| | magewares/module-mwparent | Module | Magewares | Version 1.1.0 ▾ | Install |
| | magewares/module-mwaskquestion | Module | Magewares | Version 1.0.0 ▾ | Install |

- Click "Install" and go through the installation process.

## Success

Your store is no longer in maintenance mode.

You installed:

- magewares/module-mwaskquestion

- magewares/module-mwparent

**Back to Setup Tool**

- Again, Magento will briefly take your site offline to complete the installation.
- Go to "Stores", and then "Configuration".
- Click "Ask a Question".
- Set "Enable" to "Yes", and also enter your email address.
- Click "Save Config" when you're done.

- Go to the front of your site and click through to a product. At the bottom of the screen, you'll see a box which says "Still have a question? No worries. Ask here".

- The final two words "Ask here" are a clickable link. Click these words and you'll see a form to find out more about the product:

- If you fill in the question form, you'll see the message "Thanks for contacting us with your comments and questions. We'll respond to you very soon."

## Mangoes

### MORE ADVANCED MAGENTO EXTENSIONS

As you explore the Magento Marketplace you'll find far more advanced extensions than we've seen in this chapter.

There are extensions to connect your site to other payment

gateways such as Stripe, Sage Pay and Authorize.net. There are extensions to connect you with shipping companies and tax providers. There are extensions to connect you to email marking, help desk software, and almost anything else you may need. One of the big benefits of using Magento is that there is a strong community of developers who have created solutions to just about every problem.

I will note one important thing before we wrap up our discussion of extensions.

In this chapter, we showed you how to install extensions via the admin area of your site. We did this because it's the easiest way for beginners to get started, and it doesn't require any coding. However, in a real-world environment, Magento extensions are normally installed by people with development experience who don't mind using command line tools. This process is normally faster than using the Magento UI, and doesn't require you to take your site offline. If you're new to using the command line, OSTraining has a video class available: https://ostraining.com/class/cl/.

WHAT'S NEXT?

In this chapter we showed you how to expand your site with extensions, but that's not the only thing available on the Magento Marketplace.

You can also install themes to transform the design of your site, and that's going to be our focus in the next chapter.

## MAGENTO THEMES EXPLAINED

So far in this book we've been looking at "Luma", which is the first default theme for every Magento site.

In this chapter, we'll show you how to replace Luma with another theme. First, we'll look at the Magento Marketplace, although there aren't many themes available there. Second, we'll show you other places you can look to find high-quality Magento themes.

### THEMES ON THE MAGENTO MARKETPLACE

Magento Marketplace is the best place to find extensions, but unfortunately that's not true for themes.

Unlike with extensions, there are very few themes available, whether commercial or non-commercial. At the time of writing, if you visit the themes page at https://marketplace.magento.com/themes.html and search for Magento 2 themes, you'll only get 11 results.

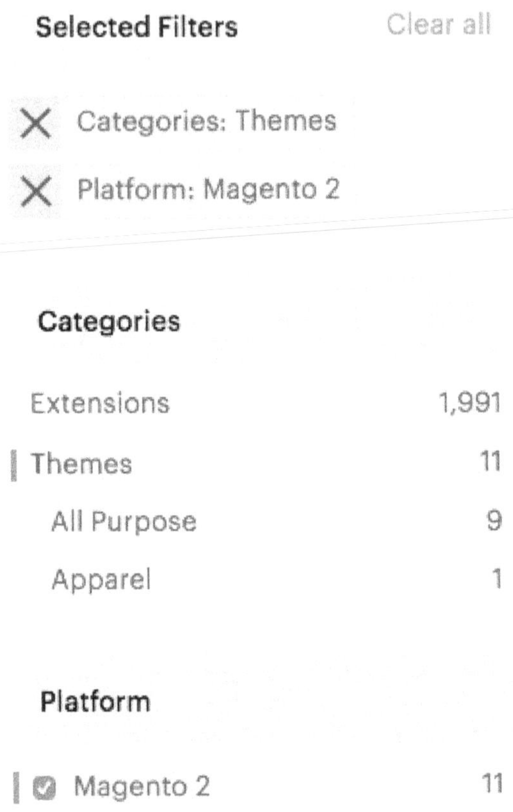

**Selected Filters** Clear all

X   Categories: Themes

X   Platform: Magento 2

**Categories**

| | |
|---|---|
| Extensions | 1,991 |
| ▍Themes | 11 |
|   All Purpose | 9 |
|   Apparel | 1 |

**Platform**

| | |
|---|---|
| ▍☑ Magento 2 | 11 |

To be honest, this is a weakness of the Magento ecosystem. There is a shortage of off-the-shelf themes. Many Magento sites do end up paying a designer to create a customized theme that is specifically designed for their needs.

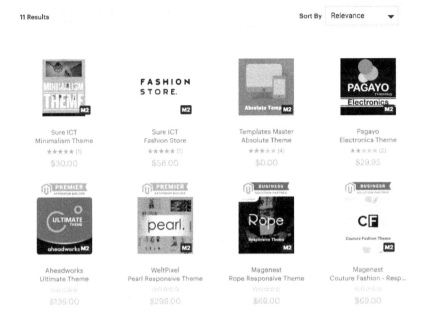

| | | | |
|---|---|---|---|
| Sure ICT Minimalism Theme | Sure ICT Fashion Store | Templates Master Absolute Theme | Pagayo Electronics Theme |
| ★★★★★ (1) | ★★★★★ (1) | ★★★★☆ (4) | ★★☆☆☆ (2) |
| $30.00 | $58.00 | $0.00 | $29.95 |
| Aheadworks Ultimate Theme | WeltPixel Pearl Responsive Theme | Magenest Rope Responsive Theme | Magenest Couture Fashion - Resp... |
| ☆☆☆☆☆ | ☆☆☆☆☆ | ☆☆☆☆☆ | ☆☆☆☆☆ |
| $139.00 | $299.00 | $69.00 | $69.00 |

Even though there aren't many themes available, it's important to see how themes are installed in Magento. In this chapter, I'll go through the process of installing the "Templates Master Absolute Theme", which is the only free theme available.

- Click "Add to Cart" and go through the checkout process.

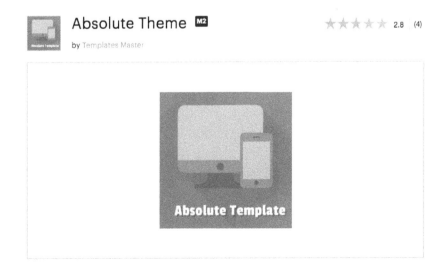

- Congrats, you've finished. The Absolute Theme is now in your Marketplace account.

## INSTALLING MAGENTO THEMES EXPLAINED

Now that we've selected the Absolute Theme, let's see how to install it.

- In your Magento site, go to "System", then "Web Setup Wizard".

- Click "Extension Manager". Yes, this is a little confusing. We do install themes via the "Extension Manager".

- When you first visit this page, you'll see a long list of modules. You may need to use the pagination to browse through multiple pages and find the theme. If your theme does not appear, click the "Sync" button on the top-right corner.

- Check the box next to your new theme:

- Click "Install".
- Go through the installation process:

## Step 3: Install

⚠ **We will take your store offline to protect shoppers during the duration of the install activity.**

We're ready to install swissup/theme-frontend-absolute to 1.1.2.

- After installing your theme, you'll see a message like the one below.
- Click "Back to Setup Tool".

## Success

Your store is no longer in maintenance mode.

You installed:

- swissup/theme-frontend-absolute

**Back to Setup Tool**

- Go back the main admin area of your Magento site. It can

sometimes be difficult to exit from the Extension Manager, so if you get stuck, enter the main admin URL for your site.

- Go to "Content", and then "Themes". Hopefully, you'll see that your new theme is available:

- Go to "Content", and then "Configuration".
- You'll see the the different parts of your store where you can configure themes. Click "Edit" in the top row:

- On this page, you can choose your new theme:

- Visit the front of your site, and you'll see the new theme in action!

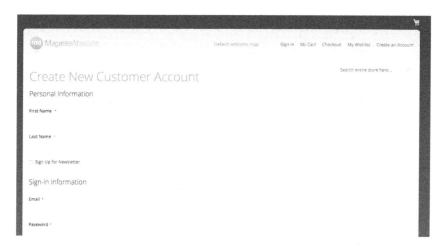

In this book, we're going to keep using Luma to talk about themes, but the Absolute theme gives you an idea of how quickly you can transform the look of your Magento site.

- Go to "Content", and then "Configuration".
- Click "Edit" in the top row.
- Choose "Magento Luma" and click "Save Configuration".

## MAGENTO THEME SETTINGS EXPLAINED

Now that we're on the Configuration page for the Luma theme, it's worth taking the time to explore our theme's settings. Remember back to the chapter called "Your First 12 Magento Tasks". In that chapter, we used this area to upload the Orangeville logo. There a lot more important theme options available here, under these seven headings:

## Other Settings

### Pagination

### HTML Head

### Header ✏

### Footer

### Search Engine Robots

### Product Image Watermarks

### Transactional Emails

For example, we can update our site's header. Have you noticed that annoying text, "Default welcome msg!", in the top-right corner of your screen? We can finally fix it now.

- Click the "Header" tab and you can change the "Welcome Text" field to something more appropriate. I changed it to "Welcome to Orangeville".

Header ✎

Logo Image    Upload

Allowed file types: png, gif, jpg, jpeg.

🟠 Orangeville

🗑

orangeville-logo_1.png
457x78, 3 KB

Logo Attribute Width

Logo Attribute Height

Welcome Text    Welcome to Orangeville

Logo Image Alt

- Click "Save Configuration", Visit the front of your site, and check the header:

Welcome to Orangeville    Sign In or Create an Account

Search entire store here...

You can also change the footer from inside this screen. Currently your footer says, "Copyright © 2013-present Magento, Inc. All rights reserved."

Copyright © 2013-present Magento, Inc. All rights reserved.

- Click the "Footer" area.

- Change the Footer text to say "Orangeville" instead of "Magento".

Footer  ✎

| Miscellaneous HTML | |
|---|---|
| | |

This will be displayed just before the body closing tag.

| Copyright | Copyright © Orangeville. All rights reserved. |
|---|---|

- Click "Save Configuration", Visit the front of your site, and check the footer bar:

Privacy and Cookie Policy

Search Terms

Contact Us

Orders and Returns

Advanced Search

Copyright © Orangeville. All rights reserved.

## MORE MAGENTO THEME CHOICES EXPLAINED

We've seen that the Magento Marketplace has an excellent choice of extensions, but a very poor selection of themes. So where do you go if you want to find a professional-quality theme?

Themeforest is a popular site with hundreds of Magento themes from many different developers: https://themeforest.net/category/ecommerce/magento.

Creative Market is a smaller alternative to Themeforest. They are also a marketplace-style site where many different designers compete to sell their themes: https://creativemarket.com/themes/magento.

There are also independent developers who sell Magento themes from their own site. A good example of this is https://argentotheme.com which sells a single, highly-customizable template.

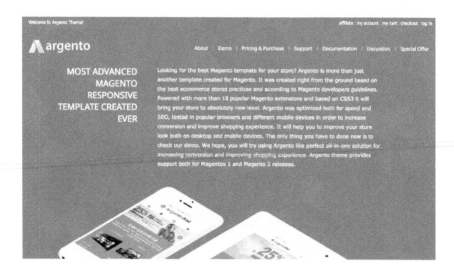

Another popular choice is http://plazathemes.com which sells four themes that are ready for Magento 2. Each theme has a demo and good documentation.

## WHAT'S NEXT?

In this chapter, we explored how to install and configure themes. If you want to learn how to modify the code for your theme, there's a video class available for OSTraining members: https://ostraining.com/class/magento-themes/.

This chapter and the previous chapter showed you how to expand your site with extensions and themes, but there's more to building a Magento site. We still don't have much control over the content on our site, whether in the main pages or the sidebar.

In the next part of the book, we'll show you how to put everything together and build a complete Magento site. In the next chapter, let's see how you add Pages with text, images and videos to Magento.

# MAGENTO PAGES EXPLAINED

In the last two chapters, you've seen how to add extensions and themes to your Magento site.

However, extensions and themes will only take you so far. To truly build a Magento site, you need to become familiar with other tools including pages, blocks and widgets.

In this chapter, we're going to show you how to add content to your site, plus build headers, sidebars and footers to show more information to customers.

## CREATING A NEW MAGENTO PAGE EXPLAINED

If you can remember all the way back to the chapter called "Your First 12 Magento Tasks", we visited the Pages area. We edited our site's existing homepage.

In the first part of the chapter, we're going to create new Pages.

- Go to "Content", and then "Pages".

You'll now see a list of Pages on your site. There are four Pages already created:

1. 404 Not Found: This can be found if you type a broken URL.
2. Home page: This controls the blank frontpage we've seen so far.

3. Enable Cookies: This text asks visitors to enable cookies if they have them disabled in their browser.
4. Privacy and Cookie Policy: This link is also in the footer menu of your site.

Notice in the image above that the "404 Not Found" has a strange entry in the URL Key column: "no-route".

What does "no-route" mean? It means that there's no fixed URL for this page. To see the "404 Not Found" page, you will need to visit a broken URL on your site. For example, try to visit this URL on your site: /privacy-policy/. This page doesn't exist, so you will see your 404 page in action:

ⓘ Not Secure | magento-⟨▂▂▂▂▂▂▂▂▂⟩.com/privacy-policy/

### Orangeville

**Vegetables**   **Fruit**   **Clothes**   **Services**   **Downloads**

# Whoops, our bad...

**The page you requested was not found, and we have a fine guess why.**

- If you typed the URL directly, please make sure the spelling is correct.
- If you clicked on a link to get here, the link is outdated.

**What can you do?**

Have no fear, help is near! There are many ways you can get back on track with Magento Store.

- Go back to the previous page.
- Use the search bar at the top of the page to search for your products.
- Follow these links to get you back on track!
  Store Home | My Account

- Click the "View" link in the same row as "Privacy and Cookie Policy".

| | 3 | Enable Cookies | enable-cookies | 1 column | All Store Views | Enabled | Sep 20, 2017 3:15:13 PM | Sep 20, 2017 3:15:13 PM | Select ▲ |
|---|---|---|---|---|---|---|---|---|---|
| | | | | | | | | | Edit |
| | 4 | Privacy and Cookie Policy | privacy-policy-cookie-restriction-mode | 1 column | All Store Views | Enabled | Sep 20, 2017 3:15:13 PM | Sep 20, 2017 3:15:13 PM | Delete |
| | | | | | | | | | View |

- You'll now see your Privacy and Cookie Policy on the front of your site.

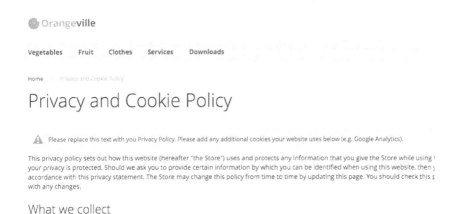

**Privacy and Cookie Policy**

Please replace this text with you Privacy Policy. Please add any additional cookies your website uses below (e.g. Google Analytics).

This privacy policy sets out how this website (hereafter "the Store") uses and protects any information that you give the Store while using your privacy is protected. Should we ask you to provide certain information by which you can be identified when using this website, then y accordance with this privacy statement. The Store may change this policy from time to time by updating this page. You should check this p with any changes.

What we collect

- Click the Back button in your browser so you return to the "Pages" screen.

Now it's time to make our own Pages. Let's create an "About Orangeville" Page for our site.

- Click "Add New Page".

- Page Title: **About Orangeville**

- Click the "Content" heading.
- Content Heading: **About Orangeville**

- Enter a couple of sentences of text into the editor screen, as in the image below. I wrote the following text:

"This is a site dedicated to the color orange.

We love orange because it's the color of Magento, and also because it's lively and fun."

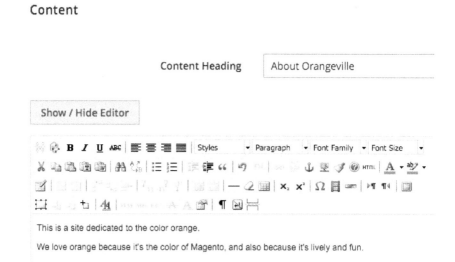

Take a few minutes to play and experiment with the Magento text editor. Many of these icons may be familiar to you from using Microsoft Word or other word processors. You'll also find similar in editors in web software such as WordPress, Drupal, Squarespace of Shopify.

Along the top row are buttons that can add style and formatting to your text. These buttons include Bold, Italic, Underline, Strikethrough, Align Left, Align Center, and Align Right.

The second row of buttons are more of a mixed bag. The first five icons are copy, plus cut-and-paste features. For example, the icon with the small Microsoft Word logo allows you to copy-and-paste directly from Microsoft Word into Magento. Further a long the row, you'll see features that include unordered lists, ordered lists and quotations. If you click the "HTML" button, you'll be able see the HTML code that creates the text for this Page.

In the third row of buttons, at least of the icons allow you to create tables. Click the first icon in this row, and you can create a table with rows, columns, padding and margins.

The fourth row is the smallest, and contains the features that you're least likely to use. Hover over the icons and you'll get a brief explanation of each feature. However, even after years of using Magento, I can never remember using most of these icons.

- Click "Save Page" in the top-right corner.
- Click the "View" link in the same row as "About Orangeville".

| | | | | | | | | | |
|---|---|---|---|---|---|---|---|---|---|
| | 4 | Privacy and Cookie Policy | privacy-policy-cookie-restriction-mode | 1 column | All Store Views | Enabled | Sep 20, 2017 3:15:13 PM | Sep 20, 2017 3:15:13 PM | Select ▼ |
| | 5 | About Orangeville | about-orangeville | Empty | All Store Views | Enabled | Jun 15, 2018 9:35:46 AM | Jun 15, 2018 9:35:46 AM | Select ▲ |

Edit
Delete
View

- What do you notice about your new Page?

# About Orangeville

This is a site dedicated to the color orange.

We love orange because it's the color of Magento, and also because it's lively and fun.

Yes, that's right. It's almost completely blank! The Page has no styling, no header, and no layout.

- Click the Back button in your browser so you return to the "Pages" screen.
- Click the "Edit" link in the same row as "About Orangeville".
- Scroll down to the "Design" area and you'll see that the "Layout" option is set to "Empty". This is why our screen is blank.

Change the "Layout" option to

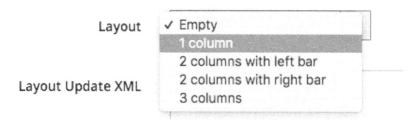

- Click "Save and Continue Edit" and visit the front of your site.
- You will now see that your Page is inside the normal design that you've seen through the book. You'll notice that there are

no sidebars on this page. This is because you chose the "1 column" layout.

- Go back to edit your "About Orangeville" page.
- Change the "Layout" option to "2 columns with right bar".

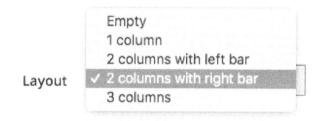

- Click "Save and Continue Edit" and visit the front of your site.
- You'll now see that there is a right sidebar visible for your new Page:

## ADDING IMAGES AND VIDEOS EXPLAINED

So far in this book we've focused on text, but it is also possible to add images, video and other content to Pages.

- Click "Edit" for your "About Orangeville" Page.

- Open the Content area.

- Place your cursor into the text area, below the content you've written. This is where your new image will be placed.

- You can add images using the tree icon in the editor box:

This is a site dedicated to the color orange.

We love orange because it's the color of Magento, and also because it's lively and fun.

- Click the tree icon, and you'll see a pop-up box.

- If you know the URL of your image, you can enter it here. However, commonly you'll want to upload an image and store it on your site. To upload an image, click the small box icon you can see below:

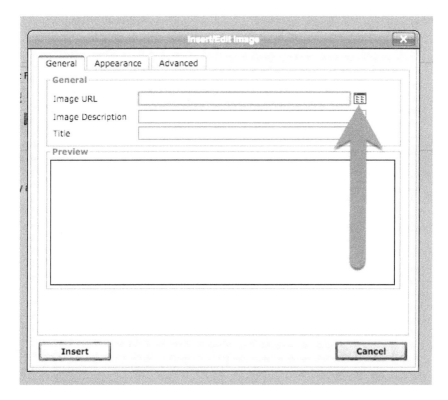

- You'll now see the image storage area inside your Magento site.

- Click the "Choose Files" button.

- Go to your Resources folder for this book, and open the /about-orangeville/ folder.

- Upload the orangeville-hq.png image.

- Click the orange "Insert File" button.

- Select the orangeville-hq.jpg and then click "Insert File" again.

- You'll go back to the pop-up box again.

- Enter "Orangeville HQ" for the "Image Description" field.

- Click the "Insert" button in the bottom-left corner:

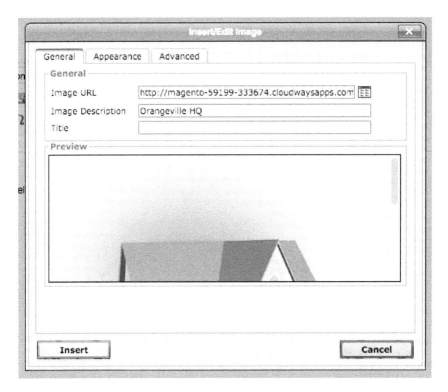

- You'll now see your image inside the main content. If you want, you can also add an explanation above the image. I wrote "This is our Orangeville Headquarters:".

Next, let's add a video to our content.

- Make a space inside your text. Place your cursor inside this space – this is where we'll place our video.
- Click the video icon.

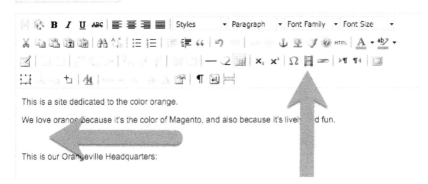

- Choose "Iframe" for the "Type".

- Enter this URL into the "File/URL" field: https://www.youtube.com/watch?v=7yRPzGaom_E

- If you've done this successfully, you'll see a video from YouTube in the "Preview" area.

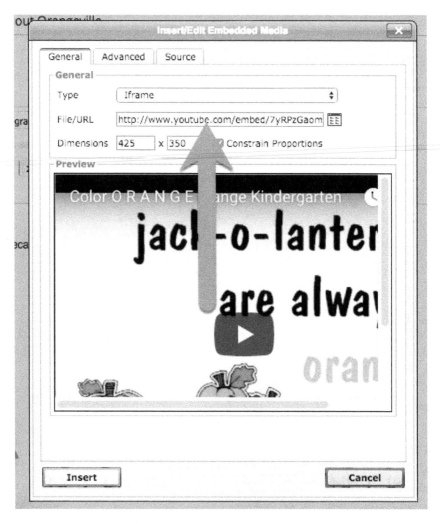

- Click the "Insert" button in the bottom-left corner.
- You won't see a preview of the video, but you will see a yellow box that indicates where your video is placed:

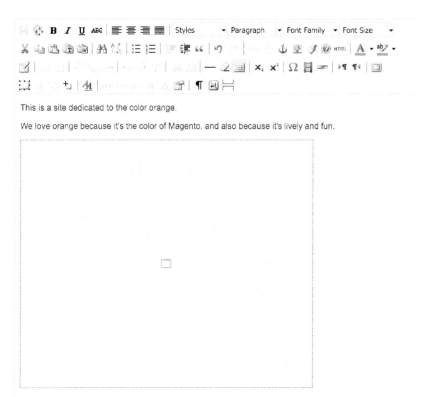

This is a site dedicated to the color orange.

We love orange because it's the color of Magento, and also because it's lively and fun.

This is our Orangeville Headquarters:

- Click "Save Page".

- Click "Visit" to see this Page on the front of your site. The YouTube video will be visible and playable inside your content.

# About Orangeville

This is a site dedicated to the color orange.

We love orange because it's the color of Magento, and also because it's lively and fun.

This is our Orangeville Headquarters:

## WHAT'S NEXT?

What did we learn from creating this new content? We learned that a "Page" consists of the main text in the center of the screen. It can contain text, images, video and more.

However, please don't place too much importance on the word "Page" here. In Magento, "Page" has a different meaning than when we normally talk about website pages. I'm always going to use the capitalized word "Page" so you know I'm specifically talking about Magento's definition of the word.

In Magento, you can't control everything on the screen when you create a "Page". Really the "Page" is only part of the puzzle, and to create a full site design, you'll need to combine it with other features that we'll talk about in the next chapter: Blocks and Widgets.

# MAGENTO BLOCKS AND WIDGETS EXPLAINED

Blocks and Widgets are the key layout features in Magento. These two features are very closely linked, and are often used together.

One way to think about Blocks is that they are mini-Pages. A Block can also contain text, images, video and more. But because Blocks are smaller, you will see them around the edges of your site. Blocks are often inserted into headers, sidebars and footers.

However, Blocks are placed using Widgets. First you create a Block, and then you use a Widget to decide where that Block will be displayed.

Let's walk you through some examples and show you how Blocks and Widgets work in Magento.

## CREATING MAGENTO BLOCKS EXPLAINED

Let's go through the process of creating our first Block. This will contain a link to the "About Orangeville" Page you created in the last chapter.

- Go to "Content", and then "Blocks".
- Click "Add New Block" in the top-right corner.

- Enter "Key Links" as the "Block Title". This is what visitors will see on the screen.

- Enter "key_links" as the Identifier. This string is what Magento uses to identify the block, but visitors will never see it.

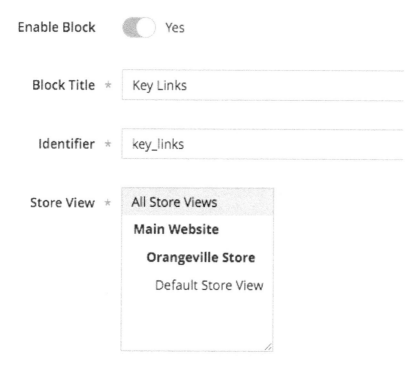

- Click the bullet icon in the editor toolbar:

- Type "About Orangeville" as a bullet point:

- Select the "About Orangeville" text and click the link icon.

- You will now see a pop-up window. Enter the URL of your "About Orangeville" page. If you're not sure what this is, you can open your Magento site in a new browser tab and find the URL, which is likely to be example.com/about-orangeville/.

- Click "Insert".

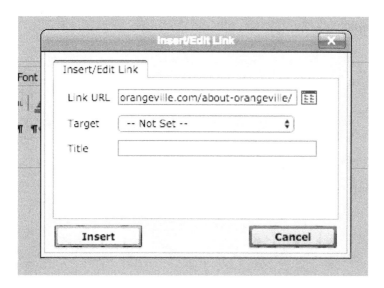

- You now have an "About Orangeville" link inside your Block:

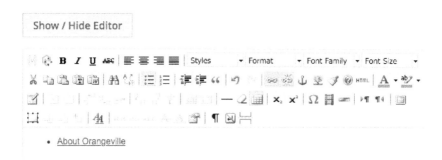

- Click "Save Block".

## CREATING MAGENTO WIDGETS EXPLAINED

We now have the challenge of placing your block into your site design. This is where Magento's Widgets come in useful. In Magento, a Block is just a piece of content. It's the Widget that controls the placement of the Block.

Remember back to the chapter called "Your First 12 Magento Tasks". Task #7 involved updating our site's homepage. We did that by placing a Widget called "Catalog Products List" into the homepage. A Widget can place our simple, new Blocks, but it can also place many other features.

- Go to "Content", and then "Widgets".
- Click "Add Widget".
- For "Type", choose "CMS Static Block".
- For "Design Theme", choose "Magento Luma".
- Click "Continue".

- Enter "Key Orangeville Links" for the "Widget Title".
- Under "Assign to Store Views", select "All Store Views".

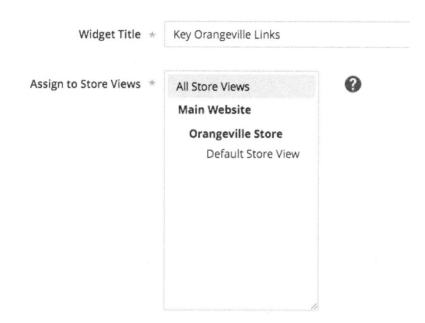

| Widget Title * | Key Orangeville Links |
|---|---|

Assign to Store Views *

All Store Views
**Main Website**
  **Orangeville Store**
    Default Store View

Next, we're going to control which URLs this Block appears on.

• Click "Add Layout Update".

## Layout Updates

Add Layout Update

• Choose "All Pages".

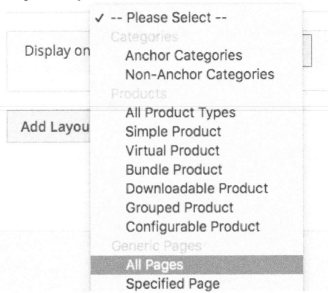

**Layout Updates**

Display on

Add Layout

- -- Please Select --
- Categories
  - Anchor Categories
  - Non-Anchor Categories
- Products
  - All Product Types
  - Simple Product
  - Virtual Product
  - Bundle Product
  - Downloadable Product
  - Grouped Product
  - Configurable Product
- Generic Pages
  - **All Pages**
  - Specified Page

- Choose "CMS Footer Links" for the "Container" option.

**Layout Updates**

| Display on | All Pages ▾ |
|---|---|

| Container | Template |
|---|---|
| CMS Footer Links ▾ | Product Link Block Template ▾ |

Add Layout Update

Both of these choices, "All Pages" and "CMS Footer Links", may not make much sense to you yet. However, we'll finish creating the widget and later in the chapter, in the section called, "Magento Widget Placement Explained", we'll explain more about why we made these choices.

Under "Layout Updates", we're going to make a second choice for where to place our widget.

- Choose "All Product Types".

- Choose "CMS Footer Links" again.

- After adding both of these options, your screen will look like the image below.

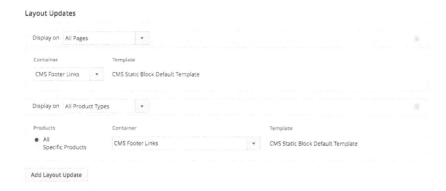

At this point, you've created the Widget and told Magento where it should appear on your site: this Widget will appear on all our Pages and all our Products.

Now it's time to choose the content of the Widget, which will be the Block you created earlier.

- Click "Widget Options" in the sidebar.

- Click "Select Block".

- Now you can choose the "Key links" block you created earlier"

Select Block...                                                    ×

| ID | Title | Identifier | Status |
|----|-------|-----------|--------|
|    |       |           | Enabled ▼ |
| 2  | Key links | key_links | Enabled |

- Click "Save".
- Visit the front of your site, and you'll see your link is now published in the footer. You created a Block with the content, and published it inside a Widget.

## CREATING BLOCKS AND WIDGETS TOGETHER

There are definitely some tricky steps as you create Blocks and Widgets. So let's try this whole process together. We'll create a second Block and place it on our site with the help of a Widget. This Block will tell people that we have a 100% satisfaction guarantee.

- Go to "Content", and then "Blocks".
- Click "Add New Block".
- Title: **Satisfaction Guaranteed**
- Identifier: **guarantee**

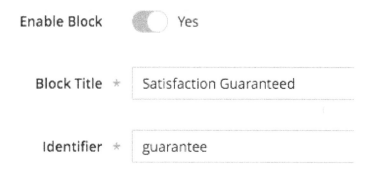

Enter text for your Block. I wrote "Here at Orangeville, your satisfaction is our top priority. If you're not happy, we'll refund your money."

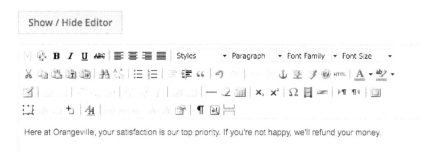

Next, we're going to upload an image for our block. We'll repeat the same process we used for the Orangeville HQ image in the last chapter.

- Place your cursor into the main content area, below the text that you just wrote.
- Click the tree icon in your editor toolbar.
- When you see the pop-up box, click the small box icon.
- Go to your Resources and the /blocks/ folder.
- Upload the satisfaction.jpg image.

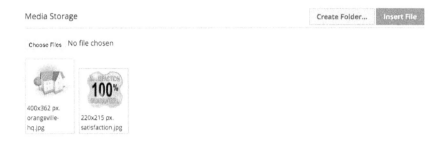

- Click "Insert File".

- Image Description: **Satisfaction Guarantee**

- Click "Insert".

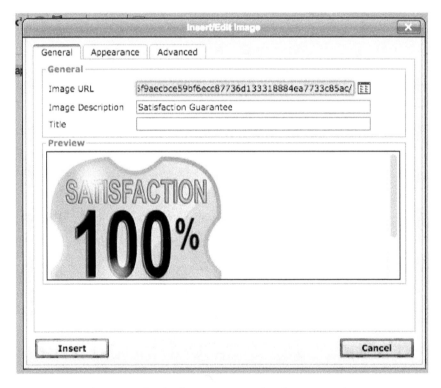

- You now have a Block that contains both text and your new image.

- Click "Save Block" to finish creating this Block.

Here at Orangeville, your satisfaction is our top priority. If you're not happy, we'll refund your money.

Next, let's create the Widget that will display this Block on our site.

- Go to "Content", and then "Widgets".
- Click "Add Widget".
- Type: **CMS Static Block**
- Design Theme: **Magento Luma**

## Settings

| | |
|---|---|
| Type ＊ | CMS Static Block ▼ |
| Design Theme ＊ | Magento Luma ▼ |
| | Continue |

- Widget Title: **Satisfaction Guaranteed**
- Assign to Store Views: **All Store Views**

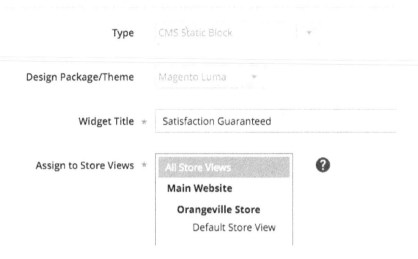

- Layout Update: **Anchor Categories**
- Container: **Sidebar Main**

- Click "Widget Options" and choose the "Satisfaction Guaranteed" Block that you just created.

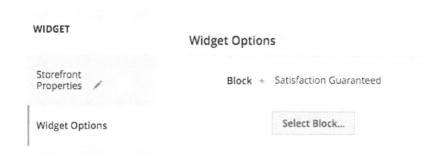

**WIDGET**

Storefront
Properties

Widget Options

**Widget Options**

Block ✳ Satisfaction Guaranteed

Select Block...

- Click "Save".
- Visit the front of your site. Click on one of the category links in the top menu. In the image below, I clicked on "Fruit". You will now see your guarantee Block in the left sidebar:

## MAGENTO WIDGET PLACEMENT EXPLAINED

One common question I get from Magento learners is about the placement of Widgets.

How do you know to choose "CMS Footer Links" or "Sidebar

Main" for the Container? After all, there are 22 different choices, as you can see in the image below.

What's the difference between "After Page Header" and "After Page Header Top"? What's the difference between "Page Footer" and "Page Footer Container"? Those names are so similar that they can definitely be confusing.

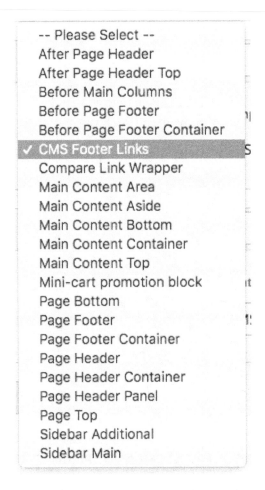

Unfortunately, there's no sure way to tell in advance, although the name will give you a good idea of the placement:

- After Page Header: This is likely to be under the main menu.

- Main Content Bottom: This is probably low down on central part of the screen, underneath our products or Page content.

- Page Top: This will appear high up on Pages, but not on Product screens.

It's worth noting that these options change, even on the same site. If you are trying to place a Block and choose "All Product Types" for your Widget's "Layout Options", then you will get a different set of choices, shown in the image below. These options provide some placements that only make sense for your product screens. For example, you now see choices that include "Product social links container" and "Review Form Fields Before". Those Widget placements don't make sense anywhere except for on Product screens.

On the other hand, this list can sometimes be much shorter. In the next part of this chapter, we'll see that some Widgets only come with three Container options.

So, there's no guaranteed way to tell exactly where your Widget will appear if you choose a particular Container. There will be some testing and experimentation involved as you test these different options.

-- Please Select --
After Page Header
After Page Header Top
Alert Urls
Before Main Columns
Before Page Footer
Before Page Footer Container
CMS Footer Links
Compare Link Wrapper
Main Content Area
Main Content Aside
Main Content Bottom
Main Content Container
Main Content Top
✓ Mini-cart promotion block
Page Bottom
Page Footer
Page Footer Container
Page Header
Page Header Container
Page Header Panel
Page Top
Product View Extra Hint
Product auxiliary info
Product info auxiliary container
Product social links container
Review Form Fields Before
Sidebar Additional
Sidebar Main

## THE DEFAULT MAGENTO LAYOUT ELEMENTS EXPLAINED

Blocks and Widgets allow you to add new items to your site's design. However, there are some elements on your site that can't easily be modified or replaced from Magento's admin interface. They look like they should be Blocks and Widgets, but Magento has not created them that way.

Here's a list of six elements that you can't easily modify:

1. The Main Menu with your product categories.
2. The search box in the top-right corner.
3. The "Compare Products" area.
4. The "My Wish List" area.
5. The footer menu with items such as "Privacy and Cookie Policy", "Search Terms", and "Contact Us".
6. The newsletter box in the bottom-right corner.

Unfortunately, all of these elements are complex and require some detailed explanation. Some of them require coding, which we try to avoid in this book. And finally, the elements may be very different, depending on the theme you choose for your Magento site.

So, I created a page with instructions for updating all of these six default elements: http://ostraining.com/books/magento/layout.

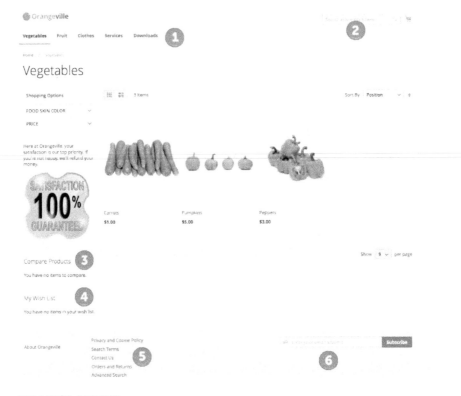

## WHAT'S NEXT?

In these last three chapters, we've talked about the design and content in Magento. We looked at Themes, Pages, Blocks and Widgets. Together, these four features help you to control the appearance of your Magento site.

In the next chapter, we'll show you how you can use your Magento site to bring in more customers.

At the end of this chapter, we've finished making all the visible changes to our Magento site that we'll make in this book. If you've followed along with every step, your site will look like the image below. As I've said many times before, don't worry if your site doesn't look like exactly like this image. So long as you understand the Magento principles that we've covered so far in this book, you're ready to move on to the next chapter.

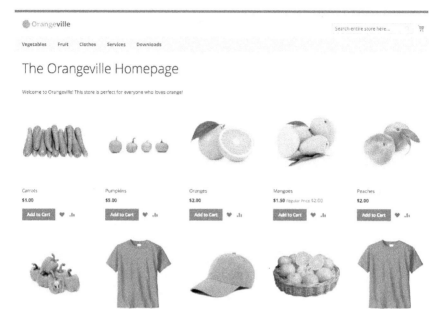

# The Orangeville Homepage

Welcome to Orangeville! This store is perfect for everyone who loves orange!

# MAGENTO MARKETING EXPLAINED

In the first 14 chapters of this book, we've focused on the technical details of your Magento store.

You've seen how to create products, collect payments and build your site.

In this chapter, we're going to turn our attention to what happens *after* your store is complete. How do you use Magento to help your marketing and drive more sales?

## MAGENTO PROMOTIONS EXPLAINED

"Promotions" is the name that Magento gives to discounts and coupons.

A discount strategy is often a fundamental part of the marketing strategy for stores. You may want to create a holiday discount, a coupon for first time customers, or a coupon just for a special audience such as your newsletter recipients or podcast listeners.

In the first section of this chapter, we're going to look at how to set up discounts and coupons in Magento.

Go to the "Marketing" menu in Magento, and you'll see the "Promotions" area has two options: "Catalog Price Rule" and "Cart Price Rules". We saw these back in the chapter called "Your First 12 Magento Tasks". In that chapter, we created a Cart Price Rule called "orange20" that gave customers a 20% discount.

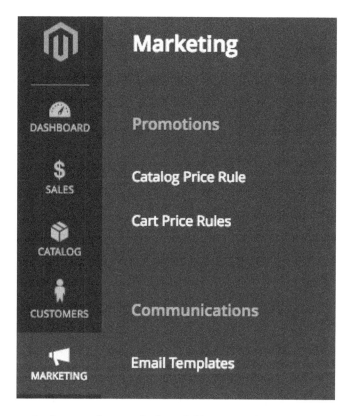

Let's remind ourselves of the difference between these two options for Promotions:

- Catalog Price Rules: these are automatic discounts. For example, you can provide an automatic 20% discount on every product in a particular category.

- Cart Price Rules: these are coupons. The customer must enter a predefined coupon code.

We created Cart Price Rules in that earlier chapter, so this time let's walk you through an example of Catalog Price Rules. In this first example, let's create a Catalog Price Rule that will automatically save customers 20% on all products in the "Fruit" category.

- Under the "Marketing" menu, click "Catalog Price Rule".

- Click "Add New Rule".

- Rule Name: **Save 20% on Fruit**

- Description: **This coupon will automatically save customers 20% on their Fruit purchases**

- Status: **Active**

- Websites: **Main Website**

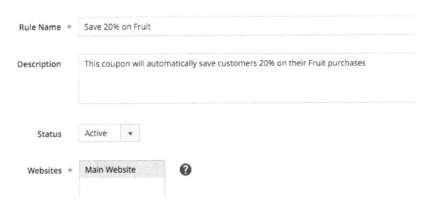

- Customer Groups: Select all the groups.

- Open the "Conditions" area.

Be warned: the user interface in this area is tricky and confusing.

I'll try to use really big arrows to try and highlight where you need to click.

- Click the green + icon.

Conditions

Conditions (don't add conditions if rule is applied to all products)

If **ALL** of these conditions are **TRUE** :

- Click the small black dots after "Category is":

Conditions (don't add conditions if rule is applied to all products)

If **ALL** of these conditions are **TRUE** :

Category **is** ... ⊗

⊕

- Click the small block icon:

Conditions

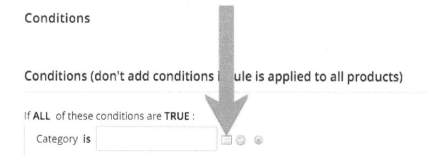

Conditions (don't add conditions if rule is applied to all products)

If **ALL** of these conditions are **TRUE** :

Category **is**

- Choose the "Fruit" Category.

- Magento will enter a number into the box at the top of the Conditions area. In the image below, the number is 10. Don't worry about this number. This number is the ID number that Magento gives to the category you've chosen.

- Open the "Actions" area.

- Discount Amount: **20**. This is the key area, where you set the discount that customers will see.

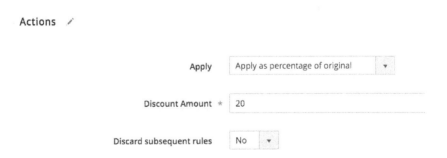

- Click "Save".

- You'll see the message "We found updated rules that are not applied. Please click "Apply Rules" to update your catalog." This means that your discount still isn't working yet.

- Click the "Apply Rules" button you see in the top-right corner.

Did I mention this process was confusing? The user interface for creating Catalog Price Rules is far from the best part of Magento. You may want to try creating discounts several times until you feel comfortable with the process.

Nonetheless, at this point, you should have a working discount. Visit the front of your site, and you'll see that Oranges, Mangoes and Peaches are all displaying a 20% discount.

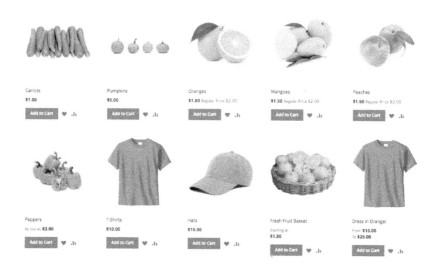

# MAGENTO EMAILS EXPLAINED

Magento emails are a topic that we also talked about in "Your First 12 Magento Tasks". In that chapter, we customized the New Account email to customers. Let's remind ourselves of how we did that by modifying another email template.

- Click "Marketing", and then "Email Templates".
- Click "Add New Template".
- You can now choose from many default emails to customize.

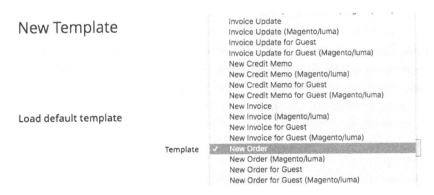

- In the example above, I'm choosing the "New Order" email.
- After choosing your email, click the "Load Template" button.

You'll now see the text that is used for Magento's automatic emails. At first glance, this text may seem impenetrable, but although the syntax is strange, most of it is written in human-readable English.

- Template Name: **Our customized New Order template**. This name is only used in the admin area of your Magento site. Customers will never see this name.

Template Information

| Template Name | * | Our customized New Order template |
| Template Subject | * | {{trans "Your %store_name order confirmation" store_name=$store.getFrontendName |

Take a look at the top of the Template Content below. One of the key lines of text looks like this:

```
<p          class="greeting">{{trans          "%customer_name,"
customer_name=$order.getCustomerName()}}</p>
```

This text is designed to automatically give a greeting to the customer. I've highlighted this text with an arrow in the image below. Let's take a look at the contents:

- **<p class="greeting">** </p> This is the HTML code for a paragraph.

- **{{ }}** This is Magento's signal that some dynamic text is being inserted. By dynamic text, I mean that the customer's name or order details  are automatically pulled from our site's records.

- **trans "%customer_name,"** This is short for "translation" and is asking Magento for your language's version of the words "Customer Name".

- **customer_name=$order.getCustomerName()** This is loading the customer's name, so if this email was to me, Magento would say "Steve" here.

| Currently Used For | Stores -> Configuration -> Sales Emails -> Order -> New Order Confirmation Template (Default Config) |
|---|---|
| Template Name * | Our customized New Order template |
| Template Subject * | {{trans "Your %store_name order confirmation" store_name=$store.getFrontendName()}} |

Insert Variable...

| Template Content * | {{template config_path="design/email/header_template"}} <br><br> <table> <br>   <tr class="email-intro"> <br>     <td> <br>       <p class="greeting">{{trans "%customer_name," customer_name=$order.getCustomerName()}}</p> <br>       <p> <br>         {{trans "Thank you for your order from %store_name." store_name=$store.getFrontendName()}} |

Now you can make a change to the email. In this example, I've replaced "Thank you for your order" with ""Thank you for you jumping on the orange train with your order". That sounds more suitable for our Orangeville store.

- Click the big, orange "Save Template" button.
- Click "Preview" in the row for your new template.

You'll see a pop-up window with your updated email template. It does lack the order and customer information, but otherwise it's an exact replica of the email that your customers will receive.

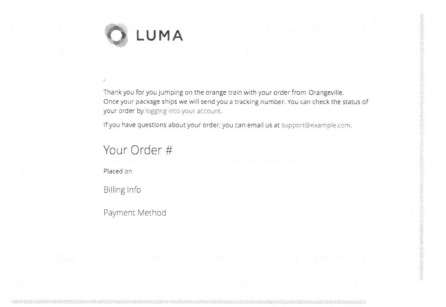

LUMA

Thank you for you jumping on the orange train with your order from Orangeville. Once your package ships we will send you a tracking number. You can check the status of your order by logging into your account.

If you have questions about your order, you can email us at support@example.com.

Your Order #

Placed on

Billing Info

Payment Method

But why – you might ask – do we still see the Luma logo on this email?

Good question. The answer is that there are several places inside Magento where you need to replace the default logo.

- Go to "Content", and then "Configuration".
- Click "Edit" in the top row.

- Open the "Transactional Emails" area.
- Upload your Orangeville logo from the resources folder.
- Click "Save Configuration".

Logo Image    Upload

Allowed file types: jpg, jpeg, gif, png. To optimize logo for high-resolution displays, upload an image that is 3x normal size and then specify 1x dimensions in the width/height fields below.

🟠 Orange**ville**

🗑

orangeville-logo_1.png
457x78, 3 KB

- Go back to "Marketing", and then "Email Templates".
- Click "Preview" for one of your customized email templates.
- Now you will see your logo on your emails:

🟠 **Orangeville**

Thank you for you jumping on the orange train with your order from Orangeville. Once your package ships we will send you a tracking number. You can check the status of your order by logging into your account.

If you have questions about your order, you can email us at support@example.com.

## Your Order #

Placed on

Billing Info

Payment Method

## MAGENTO NEWSLETTERS EXPLAINED

Magento has a newsletter system that is closely related to Magento's emails.

Perhaps without realizing it, throughout the whole course of this book, we've been open to collecting emails for our newsletter. Down in the footer area of your site, there's a newsletter box.

- Give this newsletter box a test. Enter your email and click "Subscribe".

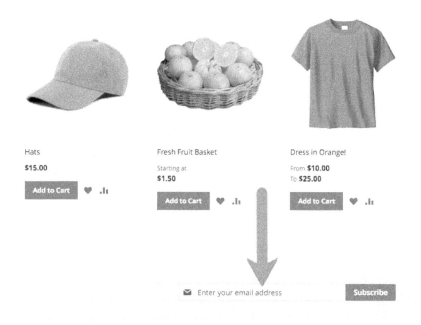

- In your Magento admin, go to "Marketing", and then "Newsletter Susbcribers". You'll see yourself listed as the first subscriber.

If you only waited for people to voluntarily subscribe themselves via the box in your site's footer, you might be waiting a long time. It is possible to add your customers to the mailing list also.

- You can add customers manually by going to "Customers", and then "All Customers".
- Click the box next to the users you want to subscribe.
- Click "Subscibe to Newsletter".

At this point, it's obligatory to mention the GDPR laws in Europe. Please check to see whether these impact you and your business and whether you feel comfortable emailing your customers. At the very least, I'd recommend offering a clear "Unsubscribe" link on your emails

When it comes to sending newsletters, Magento calls each individual newsletter a "Template" because they can be re-used multiple times. Let's see how you send a newsletter in Magento. We'll create a newsletter called "Welcome to the launch of the Orangeville Store".

- Go to "Marketing", and then "Newsletter Templates".
- Click "Add New Template".

- Template Name: This is your own private name that only your Magento admins will see.

- Template Subject: This is the email's subject that users will see in their inbox.

- Sender Name: This is the name users will see for who sent the email in their inbox.

- Sender Email: People receiving this email will see this as the "Reply to" address.

In the main body of the email, you can use all the same editor settings that we used for Pages and Blocks. All the formatting options, from bold / italic / underline to bullets and images, are available.

Follow this link to unsubscribe

{{var subscriber.getUnsubscriptionLink()}}

It's worth noting that the Widgets icon is in the top-left corner of the editor toolbar. You can use this to drop product information directly into your emails. For example, here is how you can show a single product inside your newsletter.

- Click the Widgets icon. It's the second icon from the left in the top row.
- Widget Type: **Catalog Products List**
- Title: **Carrots**
- Number of Products to Display: **1**

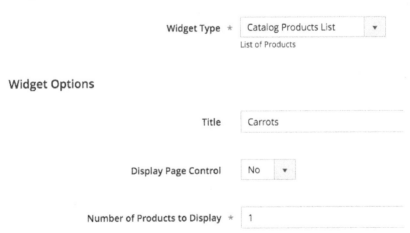

Now we have the task of selecting only Carrorts from our list of products.

- Click the green + icon in the "Conditions" area.

Conditions  ✳  If ALL  of these conditions are TRUE :

- Choose "SKU" from the list of attributes:

- Click the three black dots next to "SKU is":

Conditions  ✳  If ALL  of these conditions are TRUE :

SKU  is  ...  ⊗

- Click the small table icon:

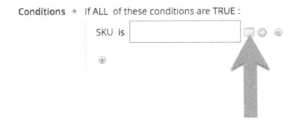

Choose the "Carrots" row from the list of products. Magento will automatically fill "FOOD101" into the SKU box.

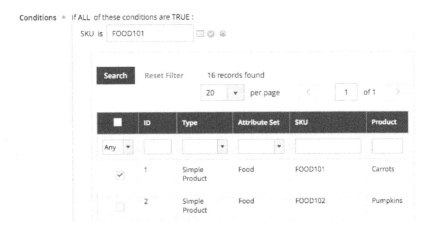

- Click "Insert Widget" in the bottom-right corner of the screen. You'll now see the Widgets icon inside your text. You can add some extra text around the Widget to complete the newsletter.

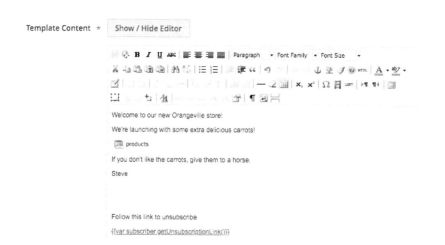

- Click "Save Template".
- Click "Preview" from the dropdown in the "Action" column.

- You'll now see a pop-up area with your newsletter.

**Store View:**  All Store Views ▼

Welcome to our new Orangeville store!

We're launching with some extra delicious carrots!

**Carrots**

1.
   Carrots
   Add to Cart
   Add to Wish List Add to Compare

If you don't like the carrots, give them to a horse.

Steve

Follow this link to unsubscribe

https://4283325f4d.nxcli.net/newsletter/subscriber/unsubscribe/

- If you like how the newsletter looks, you can click "Queue Newsletter" in the "Action" row.

- Queue Date Start: Choose a date and time to send the newsletter.

## Queue Information

- Click "Save Newsletter". You'll see that your newsletter is queued and ready for sending on the date and time you selected.

It's worth mentioning that Magento's newsletter system is OK, but it's not a core strength of the system. If you're used to more powerful commercial systems such as Mailchimp or Constant Contact, you'll find that most key features are missing. You may also need to do some coding work to improve the appearance of the newsletter, as the default layout is very plain. The main advantage of this newsletter system is that it is integrated with Magento and you can directly share products and use customer details.

At this point, it's worth noting there is a more advanced email option available inside Magento, under the "Marketing Automation" heading. This is a paid service from a company called Dotmailer.com. You will need an account with them to access any of these features. Prices start at $150 per month.

WHAT'S NEXT?

In this chapter, we've seen the marketing and promotional tools inside Magento.

However, there are other channels for driving sales to your store. In the next chapter, we'll focus on Google and show you how to optimize your site so it can be found and ranked by search engines.

# MAGENTO SEO EXPLAINED

In this chapter, we'll show you how to make some technical improvements to your site. These improvements will help search engines find and understand your content.

A quick note before we begin, please don't place too much weight on these improvements alone. You still need to create detailed descriptions for your products. You still need to persuade people to link to your site by creating interesting and useful content.

Search Engine Optimization is a large topic that involves hundreds of factors. In this chapter, we'll focus on three of those many factors: URLs, sitemaps and metadata.

## MAGENTO URLS EXPLAINED

To start this chapter, let's talk about the URLs on your Magento site. It's important that search engines can find your content on a single URL. It's also very beneficial for your visitors and search engines if your URLs are short, easy-to-remeber, and contain important keywords.

- Go to "Marketing", and then "URL Rewrites".

- Every URL on your site is stored on this screen. This includes all your Products, Pages, Category screens, and more. If you click "Edit", you can change your URL for any item on your site.

On this screen there are two really important columns: "Request Path" and "Target Path". These are both URLs for the same page, but there's a key difference:

- Request Path: This is the URL that your site visitors will see. This URL is short, clean, and human-readable.

- Target Path: This is the URL that Magento uses behind the scenes. This URL is longer, consists of multiple elements, and is hard to understand.

Although both of these URLs work, it's important to note that you don't want Google to index the Target Path URL. So whenever possible, make sure you are using the Request Path URL when linking to your Magento site.

There are a couple of other ways you can make sure Google indexes the Request Path URL.

- Go to "Stores", and then "Configuration".

- Click "Catalog" and then and then open the "Search Engine Optimization" area. On this screen, you can customize your site's URLs.

Search Engine Optimization

| | | | | |
|---|---|---|---|---|
| Popular Search Terms [store view] | Enable | | ▼ | ✓ Use system value |
| Product URL Suffix [store view] | .html | | | ✓ Use system value |
| | You need to refresh the cache. | | | |
| Category URL Suffix [store view] | .html | | | ✓ Use system value |
| | You need to refresh the cache. | | | |
| Use Categories Path for Product URLs [store view] | No | | ▼ | ✓ Use system value |
| Create Permanent Redirect for URLs if URL Key Changed [store view] | Yes | | ▼ | ✓ Use system value |
| Page Title Separator [store view] | | | | ✓ Use system value |
| Use Canonical Link Meta Tag For Categories [store view] | No | | ▼ | ✓ Use system value |
| Use Canonical Link Meta Tag For Products [store view] | No | | ▼ | ✓ Use system value |

One thing I would highly recommend doing is removing the .html from the end of your product URLs. Visit the front of your site and you'll notice that all of your products have URLs like this: http://example.com/carrots.html.

Adding .html to your sites makes no senses. This is a relic from 10 or 20 years ago when sites really were built with .html files. I would recommend that you remove the ".html" setting from both the "Product URL Suffix" and "Category URL Suffix" boxes. After you save these changes, your product URLs will look like this: http://example.com/carrots/.

I also highly recommend that you set "Use Canonical Link Meta Tag For Categories" and "Use Canonical Link Meta Tag For Products to "Yes". This "Canonical" option tells Google that the Target Path URL is the one you want indexed. It also tells Google that if this content appears on another URL, it should give that lesser priority and focus on the page withe Canonical tag.

| Use Canonical Link Meta Tag For Categories [store view] | Yes | ▼ | ☐ Use system value |
|---|---|---|---|
| Use Canonical Link Meta Tag For Products [store view] | Yes | ▼ | ☐ Use system value |

## MAGENTO SITEMAPS EXPLAINED

The Canonial tag allows Google to understand which of your site's URLs are most important. But, how do search engines find your store's pages in the first place? The answer is a sitemap. If you create a sitemap and allow search engines to find it, they will have a much better understanding of the content on your site.

Please note that the sitemap we're going to create is only for search engines. We're not about to create a human-readable sitemap for your visitors.

- Go to "Marketing", and then "Site Map".
- Click "Add Sitemap".
- Filename: sitemap.xml
- Path: /. This means the sitemap file will be located in the root of your site, rather than in a subfolder.

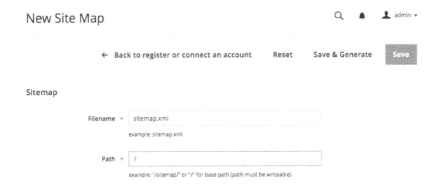

New Site Map

← Back to register or connect an account     Reset     Save & Generate     Save

Sitemap

Filename * | sitemap.xml |
example: sitemap.xml

Path * | / |
example: "/sitemap/" or "/" for base path (path must be writeable)

- Click the "Save & Generate" button.

- Click the URL for your new sitemap. I've highlighted the location of this URL in the image below.

Have you noticed I've been referring to "Google" rather than "search engines"? I've done that because Google is so dominant, and Magento does the same thing with the "Link for Google" column.

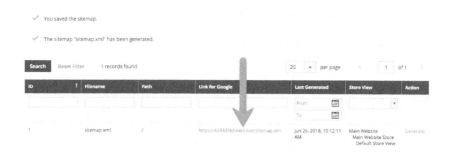

At this point, it is possible that your sitemap is not working correctly. There are some common problems that occur at this point. It's possible you'll get a 404 error when trying to check your sitemap.

If you do get a 404 error, try choosing /pub/ for your "Path" setting. This is because the files for your site are often stored in the /pub/ folder. Please note that this sitemap will still be located at example.com/sitemap.xml.

What you're looking for is a sitemap like the one shown in the image below. If you're still stuck and unable to generate a sitemap, try contacting your hosting company.

This XML file does not appear to have any style information associated with it. The document tree is shown below.

```
▼<urlset xmlns="http://www.sitemaps.org/schemas/sitemap/0.9" xmlns:content="http://www.google.co
  xmlns:image="http://www.google.com/schemas/sitemap-image/1.1">
  ▼<url>
      <loc>https://42833f4d.nxcli.net/vegetables.html</loc>
      <lastmod>2018-06-20T19:13:27+00:00</lastmod>
      <changefreq>daily</changefreq>
      <priority>0.5</priority>
    </url>
  ▼<url>
      <loc>https://42833f4d.nxcli.net/fruit.html</loc>
      <lastmod>2018-06-20T19:29:25+00:00</lastmod>
      <changefreq>daily</changefreq>
      <priority>0.5</priority>
    </url>
  ▼<url>
      <loc>https://42833f4d.nxcli.net/clothes.html</loc>
      <lastmod>2018-06-21T17:42:41+00:00</lastmod>
      <changefreq>daily</changefreq>
      <priority>0.5</priority>
    </url>
```

Once you have a sitemap like this, you can submit it to Google Search Console at https://google.com/webmasters/. If you have registered your site with Google Search Console, look for the "Sitemaps" link in the left column. On this screen, you can click "Add/Test Sitemap" and enter the URL of the sitemap you just created.

Back inside your Magento site, there are some settings available for the sitemap. You'll find these here:

- Go to "Stores", and then "Configuration".
- Click "Catalog", and then "XML Sitemap".

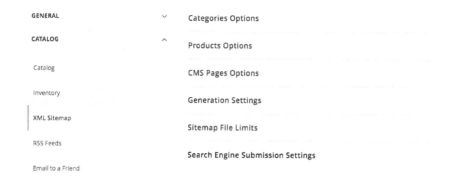

| GENERAL | ⌄ | Categories Options |
| CATALOG | ⌃ | Products Options |
| Catalog | | CMS Pages Options |
| Inventory | | Generation Settings |
| XML Sitemap | | Sitemap File Limits |
| RSS Feeds | | Search Engine Submission Settings |
| Email to a Friend | | |

There are no XML Sitemap settings that I really recommend updating. And, as I mentioned at the beginning of the book, we're only including the important information, not a mindless list of every setting. But, if you want any suggestion for this screen, it would be to set "Enable Submission to Robots.txt" to "Yes." This setting makes it slightly easier for search engines to find your sitemap, because Magneto will list the location in a file on your site called robots.txt. Search engines visit robots.txt frequently.

Search Engine Submission Settings

Enable Submission to Robots.txt [store view]  Yes ▾   ☐ Use system value

## MAGENTO METADATA EXPLAINED

So you now have clean, short URLs that use keywords related to your products.

And you have a sitemap that allows Google to find those URLs.

The next step is to create good metadata so that your products look great in Google's search results. In the image below, you can see a search result from Magento.com. This result shows two pieces of metadata:

- Meta Title: Magento: eCommerce Platform | Best Commerce Software for Selling
- Meta Description: Magento empowers thousands of retailers and brands with the best eCommerce platform and flexible cloud solutions to rapidly innovate and grow.

Magento: eCommerce Platform | Best Commerce Software for Selling ...
https://magento.com/ ▾
Magento empowers thousands of retailers and brands with the best eCommerce platform and flexible cloud solutions to rapidly innovate and grow.

Please note: don't place too much emphasis on metadata as a way to rank high in the search results. A decade ago, Google relied heavily on metadata to understand the content of your site. However, Google is now far more sophisticated and no longer needs your help. In particular, keywords have been completely abandoned by Google, who pays them absolutely no attention. However, good Meta Titles and Meta Descriptions can help your site look attractive in search results and encourage more click-throughs.

- Go to "Catalog", and then "Products".

- Open any product and scroll down. You'll see an area called "Search Engine Optimization". In here, you can change the URL for your product, and also update the Meta Title and Meta Description.

- Meta Title: This should be a concise description of your product and under 60 characters.

- Meta Description: This should be a two or three sentence product description, and ideally less than 160 characters.

Search Engine Optimization

| | |
|---|---|
| **URL Key** [store view] | carrots |
| | ✓ Create Permanent Redirect for old URL |
| **Meta Title** [store view] | Carrots |
| **Meta Keywords** [store view] | Carrots |
| **Meta Description** [store view] | Carrots |
| | Maximum 255 chars. Meta Description should optimally be between 150-160 characters |

## WHAT'S NEXT?

In the final chapter of this book, we're going to show you how to keep your Magento store safe and up-to-date.

Your website is not a work of art that is done once and then never touched again. Think of your website like a car or bicycle. Once you start using it, inevitably it will need regular maintenance.

In the next chapter, we'll talk about updates, backups, site security and other key things you should be aware of if you are in charge of running a Magento site.

# MAGENTO SITE MANAGEMENT EXPLAINED

Are you going to be responsible for maintaining your Magento site? If so, this chapter is for you. This chapter shows you how to keep your site safe, secure, and updated.

Many of you will have other people to take care of these tasks for you. You might have a web design company, colleagues in the IT department, or other experienced people to help you out. If that's you, then you can happily skip this chapter.

However, if you are the person responsible for your site, then you need to know how to keep your site safe and secure. Among other things, you need to know how to protect your site and update it to the latest version.

## MAGENTO BACKUPS EXPLAINED

It's important to keep your site secure, but even the best sites can run into problems, and even the best site administrators can make mistakes. To recover from serious problems and errors, you need to have backups. There are two main ways to make backups. Your hosting company can do it, and you can do it yourself. I recommend that you set up both options.

### Backups Made by Your Hosting Company

Many of the best hosting companies make backups for their clients. Some of the best hosts will not only make the backups but also give you the ability to restore a backup in place of the current site.

Some other hosts make the backups but require that you contact them and ask for the backup to be restored. Finally, some hosts won't make any backups at all available to you as they create backups to recover from server failure and not your mistakes.

It's important that you know the backup policy of your host, whether it's good, mediocre, or bad.

If you're using Nexcess, they allow you to set up regular backups.

- Inside the Nexcess control panel, go to "Backups", and then "Schedule".

- Click "Create Scheduled Backup".

- Nexcess allows you to set up a complete backup of your site weekly.

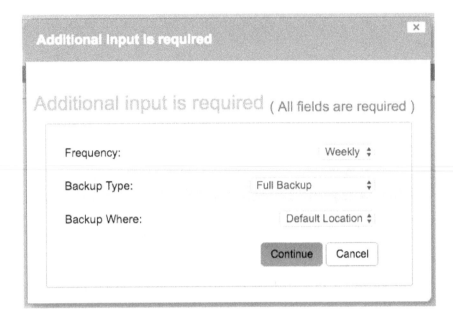

## Backups Made by You

In addition to regularly scheduled backups, you can also backup your site whenever you're doing important tasks such as updating Magento, or installing extensions. In the chapter called "Magento Extensions Explained" you saw that Magento always recommends a full-site backup before installing extensions.

Let's walk you through the process of backing up your Magento site.

- Go to "System", and then "Backups".

You'll have three choices of backup:

1. System Backup: This backs up both your code and your database.
2. Database and Media Backup: This backs up your database, plus the media folder with your images and other media files.
3. Database Backup: This backs up only your data.

We're going to take the first of these options and back up the entire site.

- Click "System Backup".

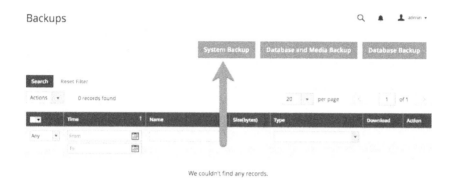

- Give your backup a very clear name. I like to use the date of the backup, and sometimes also a more detailed description, including why I'm making it.

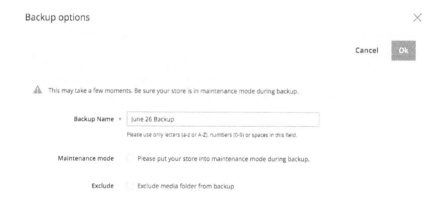

When the process is done, you'll see a message that says "You created the system backup." Your backup will be available to download in the .tgz file format.

If your site is having problems after recent changes, there is a "Rollback" button in the image above. Click the "Rollback" option, and Magento will give you the option to restore your site with your chosen backup file.

Magento also offers you the option to schedule backups. I highly recommend you take advantage of this.

- Go to "Configuration", and then "Stores".
- Click "Advanced", and then "System".
- Open the "Scheduled Backup Settings" area, and you can enable scheduled backups for your site:

## ABOUT MAGENTO UPDATES

Treat your Magento site as you treat your car.

All cars need regular maintenance, and so do all Magento sites. With a car, you need to pump up the tires, change the oil, change the battery, or do other fixes. With a Magento site, you also need to apply fixes. Fortunately the most important of these fixes can be applied automatically using Magento's update system.

Before we show you how to use Magento's update system, you need to understand what you're updating to. Magento's updates are based on major and minor version numbers, as described in the following section.

### Major Magento Versions Explained

Back in the chapter "Magento Explained," we talked a little about Magento's major version numbers. Some of the key points we mentioned are:

- You may encounter two major versions of Magento:

  ◦ Magento 1 was released in 2008.

  ◦ Magento 2 was released in 2015 and is the version we've used in this book.

- Magento 1 and Magento 2 are completely different software platforms. It is not an easy process to move from Magento 1 to Magento 2.

- More versions will be released. Eventually there will be a Magento 3 and even a Magento 4. However, those new versions are many years away, and if you build a site in Magento 2, your site should be viable for many years.

## Minor Magento Versions Explained

Minor versions are released irregularly but often and provide small fixes to existing features.

- **Numbering:** Each major version has minor versions. For example, Magento 2 has releases called 2.1, 2.2, 2.3 and so on. There are even smaller versions such as 2.1.2, 2.1.3, 2.1.4 and so on.

- **Reason for new minor versions:** Sometimes a minor version will be released to add small features, but mainly they are released to fix security problems and bugs.

- **Importance:** Is it important to use the latest minor version? Yes, absolutely. Because new minor versions are often released to fix security problems, it is vital to make sure you're using the latest version.

- **Release dates:** These versions are released approximately every one to two months, or as needed.

## What Version Do I Have?

Go to the administrator area of your site and look at the bottom-right corner of the screen. You can see what version number you currently have. In the image below, the site is at version 2.2.4

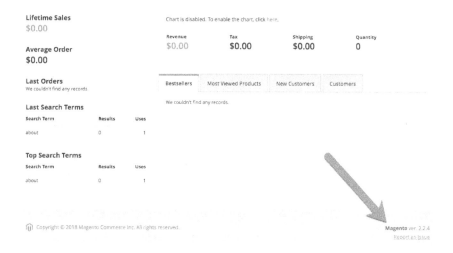

## How Do I Get Notified About Updates?

Every time you log in to your Magento site look for the notifications tab in the top-right corner. The Magento team will use these notifications to warn you about updates:

If it's a really important update, they'll also show a large pop-up window on your Magento dashboard:

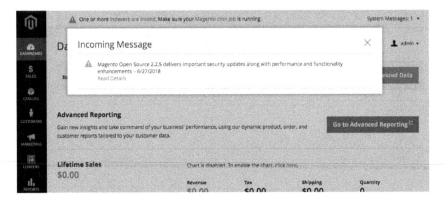

Also, I would highly recommend signing up for the Magento security newsletter. Go to https://magento.com/security/sign-up and you'll get emails for any major security updates.

## JOIN THE MAGENTO SECURITY ALERT REGISTRY

Your security is our primary concern. Occasionally our security, and yours, can be affected by outside forces. If that happens, we endeavor to make you the first to know. If you've already registered, get the latest vulnerabilities and patches for Magento: Visit the Magento Security Center.

* First Name:

* Last Name:

* Email Address:

## HOW DO I UPDATE MAGENTO?

You can update Magento with just a couple of clicks inside your site's administrator area. The process is similar, but slightly different from the one we used for installing Magento extensions in the chapter called "Magento Extensions Explained".

- Go to "System", and then "Web Setup Wizard". Please

remember that not every hosting company will allow Magento users to access the "Web Setup Wizard" area. Some hosting companies do disable access for security reasons. If you are not able to proceed at this point, please contact your hosting company.

- Click "System Upgrade".

Welcome to the Magento Setup Tool. Please choose a task below.

**Extension Manager**
I want to manage my extensions and themes

**Module Manager**
I want to manage my modules

**System Upgrade**
I want to upgrade my Magento Admin version

**System Configuration**
I want to change my Magento system configurations

- If your Magento site doesn't still have your connection from the "Magento Extensions Explained" chapter, enter your Public and Private API Keys from the Magento Marketplace.

**Magento** Marketplace

To upgrade or install purchases, enter your access keys

**Need to find your keys?**

1. Go to your Magento Marketplace account page.
2. On the "Access keys" page, copy your public and private keys.
3. Enter keys below:

⋆ **Public Access Key**

c9c8e83581856e40e36a2e925

⋆ **Private Access Key**

••••••••••••••••••••••••••••••

**Sign in**

- Magento will now search to find a newer version of the core software.

- Click "Next" if Magento finds that a new version is available for you.

| System Upgrade | Readiness Check | Create Backup | System Upgrade |

**Step 1: Select Version**

ⓘ   Your Magento version is Version 2.2.4 CE. You are about to upgrade to a newer version.

| | |
|---|---|
| Magento Core Components | Version 2.3.0-alpha CE (latest) (unstable version) |
| Show All Versions | ☑ |

- Magento will now take you to the Readiness Check that we

covered in depth in "Magento Extensions Explained". Please check that chapter for advice if your site doesn't meet Magento's criteria.

## Step 2: Readiness Check

Let's check your environment for the correct PHP version, PHP extensions, file permissions and compatibility.

**Start Readiness Check**

- Magento will now offer to take a backup of your site. If you choose to take a backup, this may take a while because the default choice is to backup your code, media, and the database.

- After the backup is done, you'll see the message: "Completed! You can now move on to the next step."

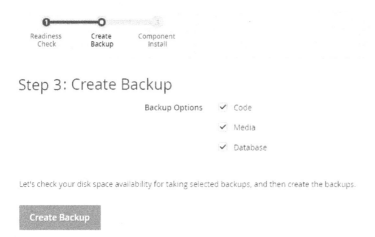

## Step 3: Create Backup

Backup Options  ✔ Code
✔ Media
✔ Database

Let's check your disk space availability for taking selected backups, and then create the backups.

**Create Backup**

- Now you'll be in Step 4, when you can click "Upgrade".

System Upgrade

Step 4: System Upgrade

We're ready to upgrade magento/product-community-edition to 2.0.1.

Upgrade

- Once the process is complete, you'll see this "Success" message. Now it's time to test your site to make sure everything is still working smoothly after the update.

## Success

Your store is no longer in maintenance mode.

You upgraded:

- magento/product-community-edition

**Back to Setup Tool**

## MAGENTO CRON JOBS EXPLAINED

When you first set up your Magento site, you may have seen

this message: "One or more indexers are invalid. Make sure your Magento cron job is running."

Cron jobs are an essential tool for keeping your Magento site healthy. An eCommerce store requires many different tasks to run every day:

- Generate sales and tax reports.

- Update sitemaps.

- Send scheduled newsletters.

- Index your products so visitors can search and find them.

- Remind users about subscriptions that are renewing or expiring.

Some of these tasks happen every five minutes. Some of these tasks happen once a day. But all of theses tasks need to be run on a regular basis. Magento uses **cron jobs** to make these tasks run.

There are three cron jobs that you must set up on your server. Each of these three cron jobs will trigger a different file, and each file will run several tasks.

Unfortunately, there's no easy way to show how to set up cron jobs in a way that will be useful to most readers. Each hosting company has a different approach, so I highly recommend that you discuss this with your hosting company. Nonetheless, we've tried to share some useful links at our website: https://ostra.in/cron-jobs.

There are some configuration options available for cron jobs inside your Magento site.

- Go to "Stores", and then "Configuration".
- Click "Advanced", and then "System".
- Open the "Cron (Scheduled Tasks)" area.
- You'll see three cron configuration options:

  - index: Tasks in this group will start every minute.
  - default: Tasks in this group will start every 15 minutes.
  - ddg_automation: This the commercial Dotmailer application that we mentioned in the chapter "Magento Marketing Explained".

Cron (Scheduled Tasks)

For correct URLs generated during cron runs please make sure that Web > Secure and Unsecure Base URLs are explicitly set. All the times are in minutes.

  ⊙ Cron configuration options for group: index

  ⊙ Cron configuration options for group: default

  ⊙ Cron configuration options for group: ddg_automation

Open up any of these three settings, and you'll see that you can customize the default options.

It's worth noting that these are the *minimum* times. If you go into your hosting company's control panel and set up cron jobs to run every 30 minutes, then the settings here won't matter. In that situation, the only way these settings would have an impact is if you increase these minimum times to more than 30 minutes. For an excellent guide to all these settings, and everything you might want to know about Magento cron jobs, visit https://ostra.in/cron-tutorial.

## ⊙ Cron configuration options for group: index

| | | |
|---|---|---|
| Generate Schedules Every [global] | 1 | ✓ Use system value |
| Schedule Ahead for [global] | 4 | ✓ Use system value |
| Missed if Not Run Within [global] | 2 | ✓ Use system value |
| History Cleanup Every [global] | 10 | ✓ Use system value |
| Success History Lifetime [global] | 10090 | ✓ Use system value |
| Failure History Lifetime [global] | 10090 | ✓ Use system value |
| Use Separate Process [global] | Yes | ✓ Use system value |

# WHAT'S NEXT?

---

Congratulations! You've reached the end of the main portion of Magento 2 Explained!

You're now ready to go out and improve your Magento skills.

What should you do next?

- **Practice**. The only way to get better at Magento is to build Magento sites. Decide on your first Magento project and start practicing.

- **Practice now**. You will forget most of what you've read in this book. That's human nature and doesn't make us bad teachers or you a bad learner. The longer you wait to practice Magento, the more you'll forget. Why not start right away?

- **Learn more**. We guarantee that there are things you will come across while using Magento that haven't been included in this book. This book has only a limited number of pages, and we've tried to focus on only the most important things about Magento.

## ARE YOU STUCK ON A MAGENTO PROBLEM?

One of the great things about Magento being so popular is that almost every problem you run into has been encountered by other people. Many of those people will have asked for or posted a solution to their problem online.

If you ever get stuck, here are the first places you should go to for help:

- **Contact us**: Get in touch by emailing books@ostraining.com. We can't guarantee an answer to everything, but we'll try and point you in the right direction.

- **Use Google**: If you get an error message or encounter a problem, type it directly into a search engine, and there's a good chance you'll find a solution.

- **Use the Magento help forums**: https://community.magento.com. The Magento forums have millions of posts, so you can find a lot of solutions. Search for a solution to your question, and if you don't find it, write a new post. There's sure to be someone who can help you.

- **Join the Magento community**: Whether you attend a local Magento event, post solutions you find on the Magento Community forum, or even say thank you to someone who's helped you, there are many easy ways to become part of the Magento community. The more you rely on Magento for your website or your business, the more it can benefit you to become part of the community. Visit https://magento.com/events for an event near you, or online.

I hope to see you around in the community, and we wish you all the best in your use of Magento!

www.ingramcontent.com/pod-product-compliance
Lightning Source LLC
La Vergne TN
LVHW022301060326
832902LV00020B/3212